1-99

D1743690

Cover illustration: Wearing the colourful markings of a prewar era, two F-105D Thunderchiefs from the 53rd TFS/36th TFW (60-0527 is in the foreground) wing through German skies in 1961. Stationed at Bitburg AB, the Thunderchiefs were a key element of NATO air defences. (Donald L. Jay)

1. The last Air National Guard Thunderchief flight. Followed by the F-4D Phantom which replaced it in the Georgia ANG, F-105F 63-8299, with the wing tank reading 'Thuds Forever' in 8in red, white and blue letters, heads for NAS Patuxent River and retirement. Soon after this, the Air Force Reserve flew the last 'Thud' mission. Though many F-105 airframes survive, it is unlikely that any will ever be flown again. (Don Spering/AIR)

WARBIRDS ILLUSTRATED No 49

F-105
Thunderchief

ROBERT F. DORR

a&
ap

ARMS & ARMOUR PRESS
London   New York   Sydney

Introduction

First published in Great Britain in 1988
by Arms & Armour Press Ltd.,
Artillery House, Artillery Row, London SW1P 1RT.

Distributed in the USA by Sterling Publishing Co.
Inc., 2 Park Avenue, New York, NY 10016.

Distributed in Australia by Capricorn Link
(Australia) Pty. Ltd., P.O. Box 665, Lane Cove,
New South Wales 2066.

British Library Cataloguing in Publication data:
Dorr, Robert F.
F-105 Thunderchief. – (Warbirds illustrated; v. 49).
1. Thunderchief (Fighter planes) – History
I. Title.   II. Series
623.74'63   UG1242.F5

ISBN 0-85368-901-6

Edited and designed by Roger Chesneau.
Typeset by Typesetters (Birmingham) Ltd.
Printed and bound in Great Britain by The Bath
Press.

◄2
2. 'Thud on the boom'. Vietnam was the first war in
which air-to-air refuelling was employed routinely on
combat missions. The 'boomer' who fed fuel into the
'Thud' looked down at it from this angle and guided
the KC-135's boom into the F-105's receptacle. (Via
Eric Renth)

The Republic F-105 Thunderchief could seem graceful at times and was as 'tough as a tin can', especially when the North Vietnamese tried to bring it down, but above all it was the ultimate expression of size and brute force in a jet fighter aircraft. At 64ft 10in it was longer by half a foot than a PBY Catalina flying boat, and its maximum take-off weight of 52,838lb was only a few pounds less than that of a Boeing B-17G Flying Fortress. Originally designed for the 15,000lb thrust Pratt & Whitney J57 engine, the Thunderchief from the third airframe onward was in fact propelled by the more powerful, 17,200lb Pratt & Whitney J75-P-19W, with an afterburner that produced some of the loudest and most powerful take-offs of any warplane ever built. As one pilot put it, the Thunderchief was living proof that, given enough power, a brick could fly. Pointed nose, yes. Sleek, yes. But pilots were always aware of the enormous weight beneath them and, because their aircraft could make a mighty sound if it ever came abruptly into contact with the ground, they called it the 'Thud'. Of twelve airmen to earn the Medal of Honor in South-East Asia, only two flew fighters, both F-105F Wild Weasels.

During the 1965–68 'Rolling Thunder' campaign against North Vietnam, two American fighter Wings bore the brunt of the long and frustrating fight against a bitterly entrenched enemy. The 355th Tactical Fighter Wing (TFW) at Takhli produced men like Colonel Jack Broughton, the intrepid West Pointer who was forty-five years of age when he pitted his supersonic fighter-bomber against Hanoi's missiles, MiGs and anti-aircraft guns; and Captain Max Brestel, who shot down two MiG-17s on a single mission. The 388th TFW at Korat, dubbed the 'Avis Wing' after the advertising slogan about a car rental company which tried harder because it was Number Two, had men like 1st Lt. Karl Richter who got a MiG and flew at least 210 combat missions – more than twice the requirement – before he was lost on his final trip to the Hanoi region. Most men were grateful enough to complete the requisite 100 combat missions in the 'Thud'. The toughness, durability and staying power of their aeroplane helped them to do it, but it was no easy task: there were even statistics which 'proved' that it couldn't be done. Skyhawks, Crusaders, Phantoms and other aircraft also fought the war 'up North', but none paid a higher price than the 'Thud' and the men who flew it.

On the pages which follow, all manner of 'Thuds' are presented in pictorial form, from the YF-105A prototype to the F-105G Wild Weasel which challenged Hanoi's missile network. They fly no longer, for the Thunderchief is now a museum piece, a part of history – but the story cannot be forgotten as long as men are tasked to fly and fight. This book is dedicated to Richter, who refused to go home as long as there was another mission to fly.

Many of the photographs are seen here for the first time. Any mistakes are the responsibility of the author, but the volume would not have been possible without the generous help of others. I especially want to thank David Anderton, Col. Jack Broughton, John L. Frisbee, Clyde Gerdes, Joseph G. Handelman DDS, Marty J. Isham, Donald L. Jay, Donald S. McGarry, Peter B. Mersky, Blake Morrison, Dave Parsons, Douglas Remington, Eric Renth, Col. Dave Roeder, Brian C. Rogers, Harrison Rued, Don Spering/AIR, Douglas R. Tachauer, Philip A. Tachauer and Nick Williams.

Near my home, there is a 'Thud' on a pole, one of those 'gate guardians' which once flew and fought in smoke-filled skies. And I still say that the F-105 looks as though it's boring through the sky at Mach 2 even when it's sitting on the ground!

Robert F. Dorr

▲3 ▼4

3. Republic test pilot Russell M. (Rusty) Roth lifts off from Edwards AFB, California for the 45-minute maiden flight of the first YF-105A (54-0098), 22 October 1955. The air intakes and tail shape differ from those on the production F-105B that was to follow. (Via David A. Anderton)

4. The first two F-105s were powered by J-57 engines rather than the J75 powerplant intended for the production F-105B. The second YF-105A (54-0099) first flew at Edwards AFB on 28 January 1956 and had the name 'Thunderchief' painted on the forward fuselage. (Via David A. Anderton)

5. The second YF-105A, photographed during an early test flight in 1956; the early-style refuelling probe is extended. The Thunderchief was designed as a supersonic nuclear bomber, with an internal bomb bay. (Via David A. Anderton)

▲ 6

6. The No. 3 F-105B (54-0102) at Edwards AFB, California, on 20 June 1958. The B-model introduced the production J75 engine, revised air intakes exhaust nozzle, and a large vertical tail. (Via Marty J. Isham)

7. Early F-105B fighters (57-5779 in the foreground) await delivery at the Farmingdale, Long Island plant. The Indian-head insignia of the 4th Tactical Fighter Wing is visible behind the 'buzz number' on the forward fuselage. (Via Blake Morrison)

8. F-105B 57-5836 with 500lb bombs; the aircraft has a Tactical Air Command (TAC) badge on its tail. Early F-105s appeared in natural metal but later, under Operation 'Look-Alike', they received a

covering of anodized aluminium. (Via Blake Morrison)

9. After a two-seat strike F-105C was cancelled in its design stages, the F-105D flew on 9 June 1959, introducing a new fire control system and a slightly longer fuselage. These aircraft belong to the 4526th Combat Crew Training Squadron and are seen over the Nellis, Nevada, range in 1961. (Via Marty J. Isham)

10. The 36th TFW at Bitburg AB, Germany, re-equipped with F-105Ds on 12 May 1961 and the 49th TFW at Spangdahlem followed. Here, with 60-0464 in the foreground, Bitburg 'Thuds' fly in formation in European skies. The tail stripes are (from the top) red, blue and yellow. (Via Marty J. Isham)

▼ 7

U.S. AIR FORCE
FH-836

8▲

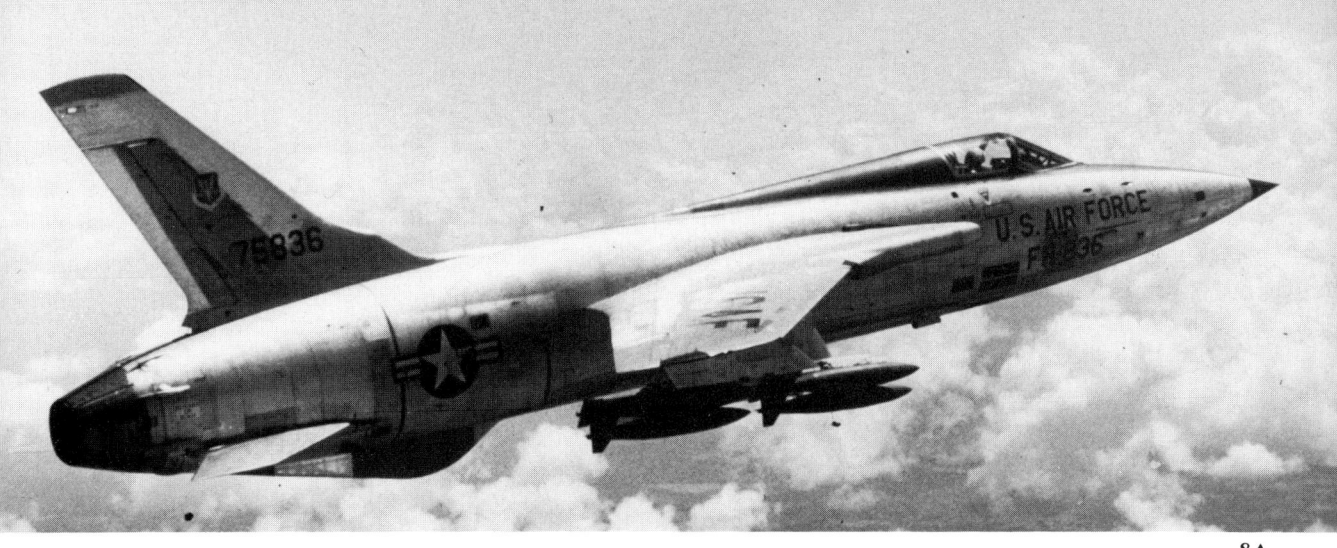

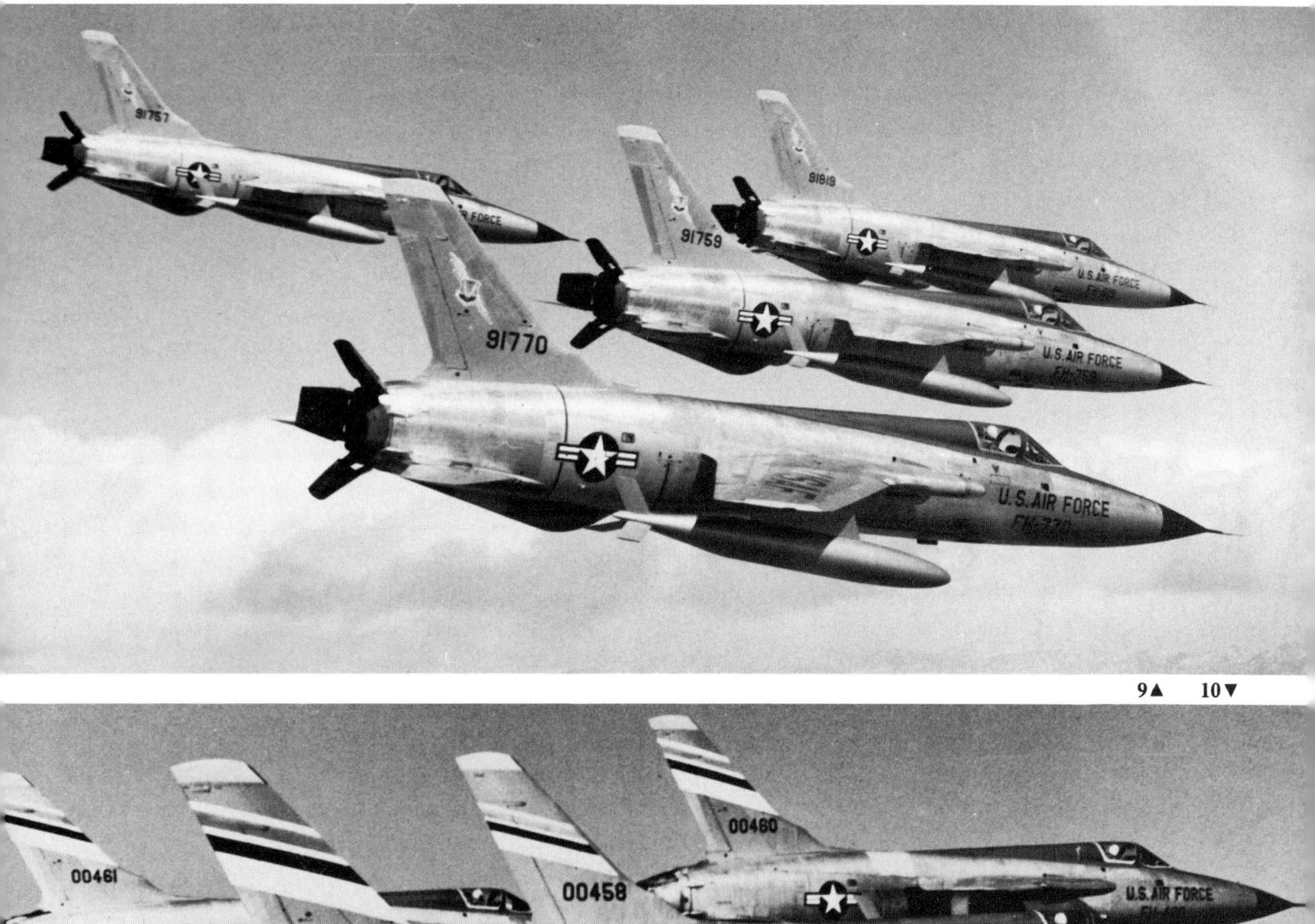
91757
91819
91759
91770
U.S. AIR FORCE
U.S. AIR FORCE

9▲ 10▼

00461
00458
00460
00464
U.S. AIR FORCE
U.S. AIR FORCE
U.S. AIR FORCE

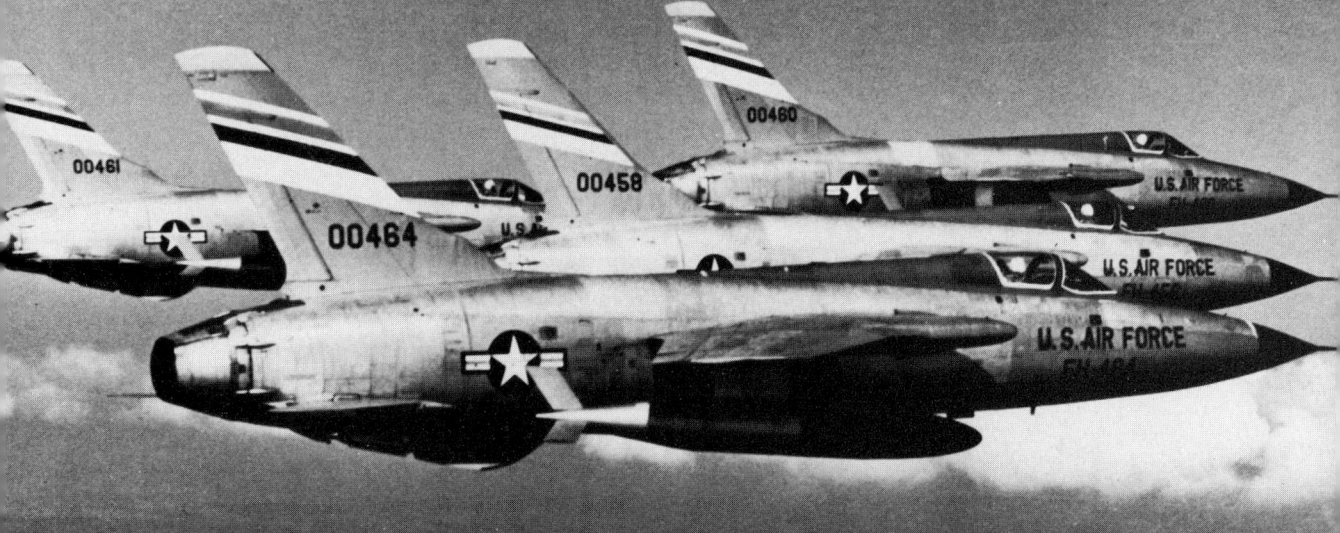

▲11

11. The other Thunderchief wing to serve in Europe for a time was the 49th TFW. This F-105D had a Wing crest with red, yellow and blue stripes on the tail and in the form of a barely discernible band around the nose. (Via Marty J. Isham)

12. F-105D Thunderchiefs 59-1771 (right) and 59-1743 of the 4520th Combat Crew Training Wing flying near Nellis AFB, Nevada, in 1961. (Via Marty J. Isham)

13. Taxiing with its canopy open, F-105D 59-1721 reveals the classic lines of the largest single-engine fighter ever built. (Author)

14. F-105D 59-1750 of the 4520th Combat Crew Training Wing in flight near Nellis AFB in 1961. (Via Marty J. Isham)

15. By 1965 Thunderchiefs had the dull silver appearance caused by the coating applied under Project 'Look-Alike', and the Air Force was no longer using the 'buzz number' on the nose. This is F-105D 62-4257, at Wright-Patterson AFB, Ohio, 15 May 1965. (Clyde Gerdes)

▼12

▼13

16. The USAF's *Thunderbirds* flight demostration team usually flew the 'hottest' aircraft on the inventory, but the Thunderchief seemed too much for them. For a brief period in 1964 the *Thunderbirds* had nine F-105Bs with the paint scheme shown, the usual variation of the team's red, white and blue pattern. The team soon returned to the F-100. (Via David A. Anderton)

17. An early photograph of the No. 4 F-105B airframe, 54-0103, undergoing developmental testing at Republic's Farmingdale, Long Island facility. With designer Alexander Kartveli as its guiding light, Republic had produced the P-47 Thunderbolt and F-84 Thunderjet before the '105' came along. (Via Marty J. Isham)

18. Seen here at Nellis AFB in 1961, F-105D Thunderchief 59-1773 belonged to the 4520th Combat Crew Training Wing. The 'buzz number' (FH-773), supposedly intended to permit citizens to see and report any Air Force craft illegally 'buzzing' at low level, was found on the 'Thud' until mid-1965. (Via Marty J. Isham)

19. The F-105E, like the F-105C, was a two-seat 'Thud' that was not built. The two-seat F-105F, flown on 11 June 1963, was both fighter-bomber and transition trainer; 143 were delivered (like 62-4412 here) before anyone saw a role for them in South-East Asia. (Via Blake Morrison)

20. The second F-105F two-seater kicks up a storm of exhaust gases at a TAC air base in the United States. The ground crewman at right is connected to the Thunderchief's pilot via an umbilical intercom wire which permits direct conversation while the 'Thud' starts up. (Via Marty J. Isham)

▲16　▼17

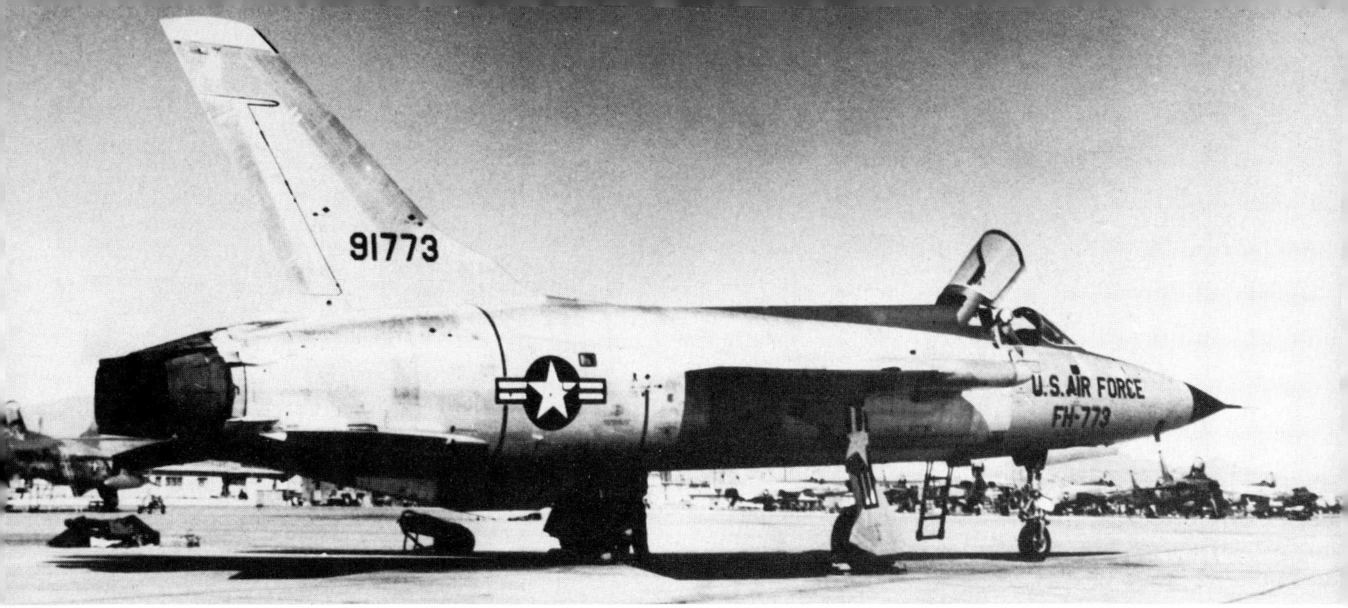
91773
U.S. AIR FORCE
FH-773

18▲

U.S. AIR FORCE
FH-412
24412

19▲ 20▼

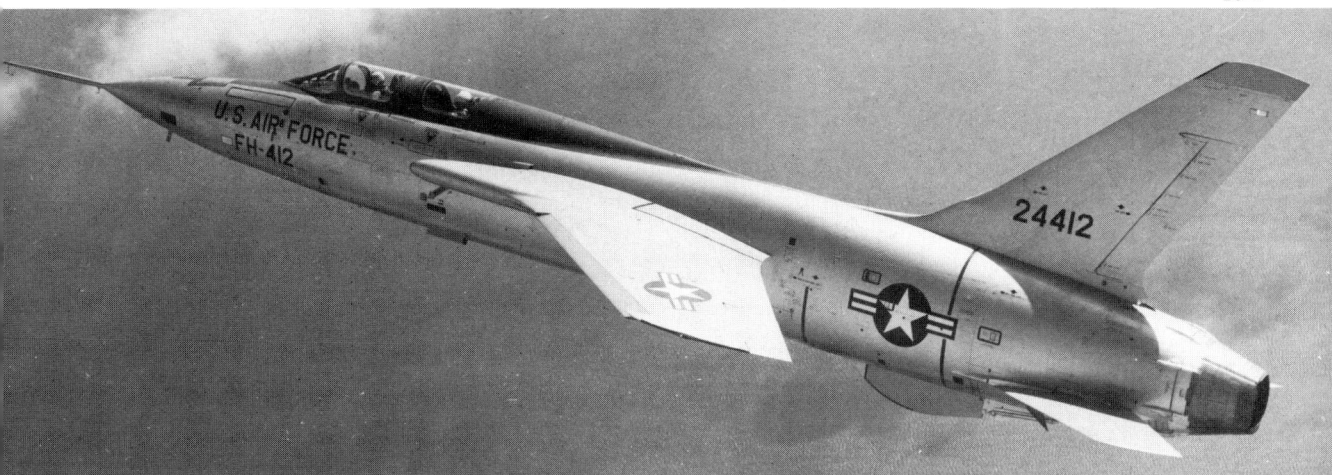

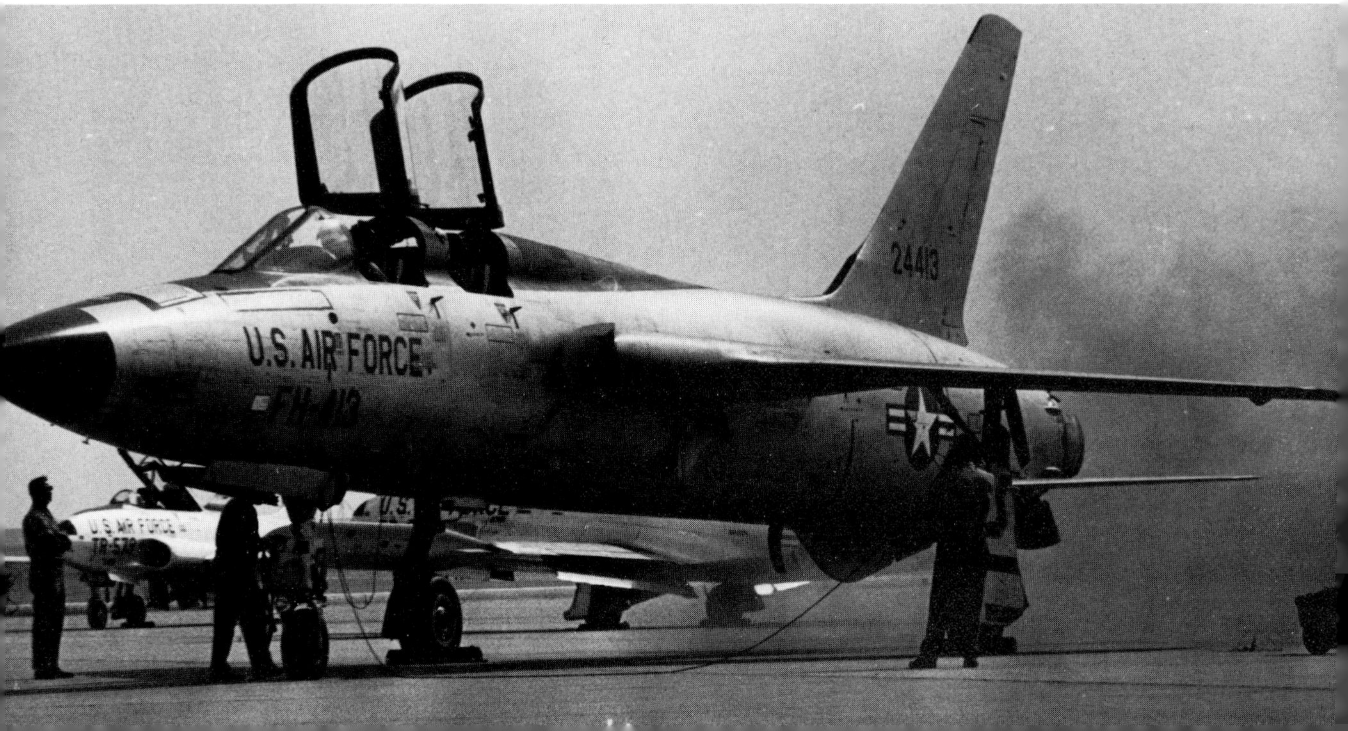
U.S. AIR FORCE
FH-413
24413

▲21

21. Americans first went into South-East Asia in 1961 and the F-105 Thunderchief began to arrive in the region in 1964. In this early formation over Thailand, two F-105D Thunderchiefs keep up a loose diamond with two RF-101C Voodoos. (Lt. Col. John R. Evans)

22. Two F-105D Thunderchiefs head for North Vietnam in 1966, during the time of changeover from natural metal to camouflage finish. This was the period when Secretary of Defense Robert

McNamara denied that there was a bomb shortage, even though these 'Thuds' carry only three 750-pounders each. (Via Eric Renth)

23. F-105D Thunderchief 58-1173 in natural metal at Eglin AFB, Florida, in the mid-1960s. (Clyde Gerdes)

24. F-105D 59-1725 in an early camouflage scheme, with the abbreviation 'USAF' and the tail number in black. The national insignia on this aircraft appears at an unusally low location on the fuselage. (USAF)

▼22

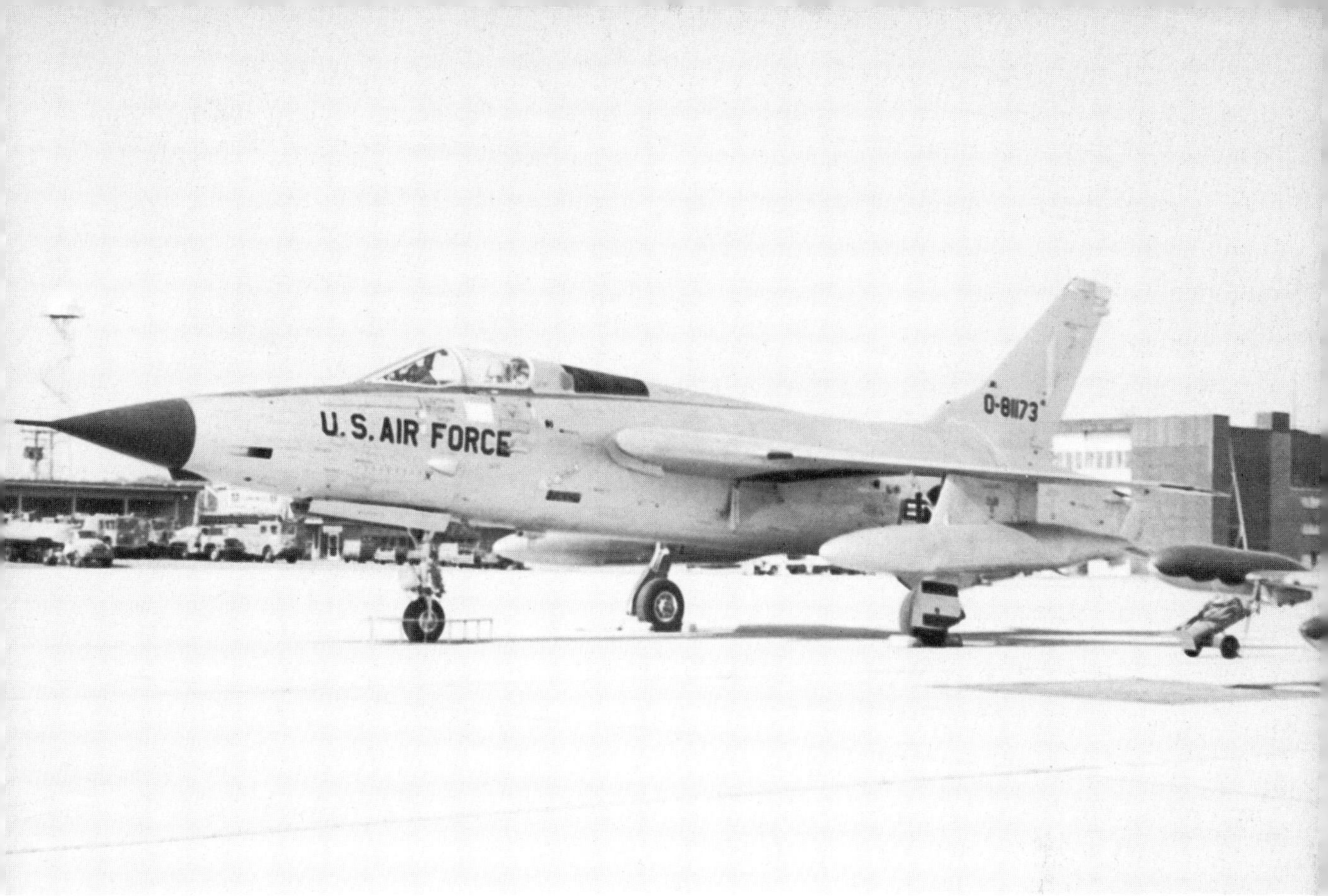

23▲ 24▼

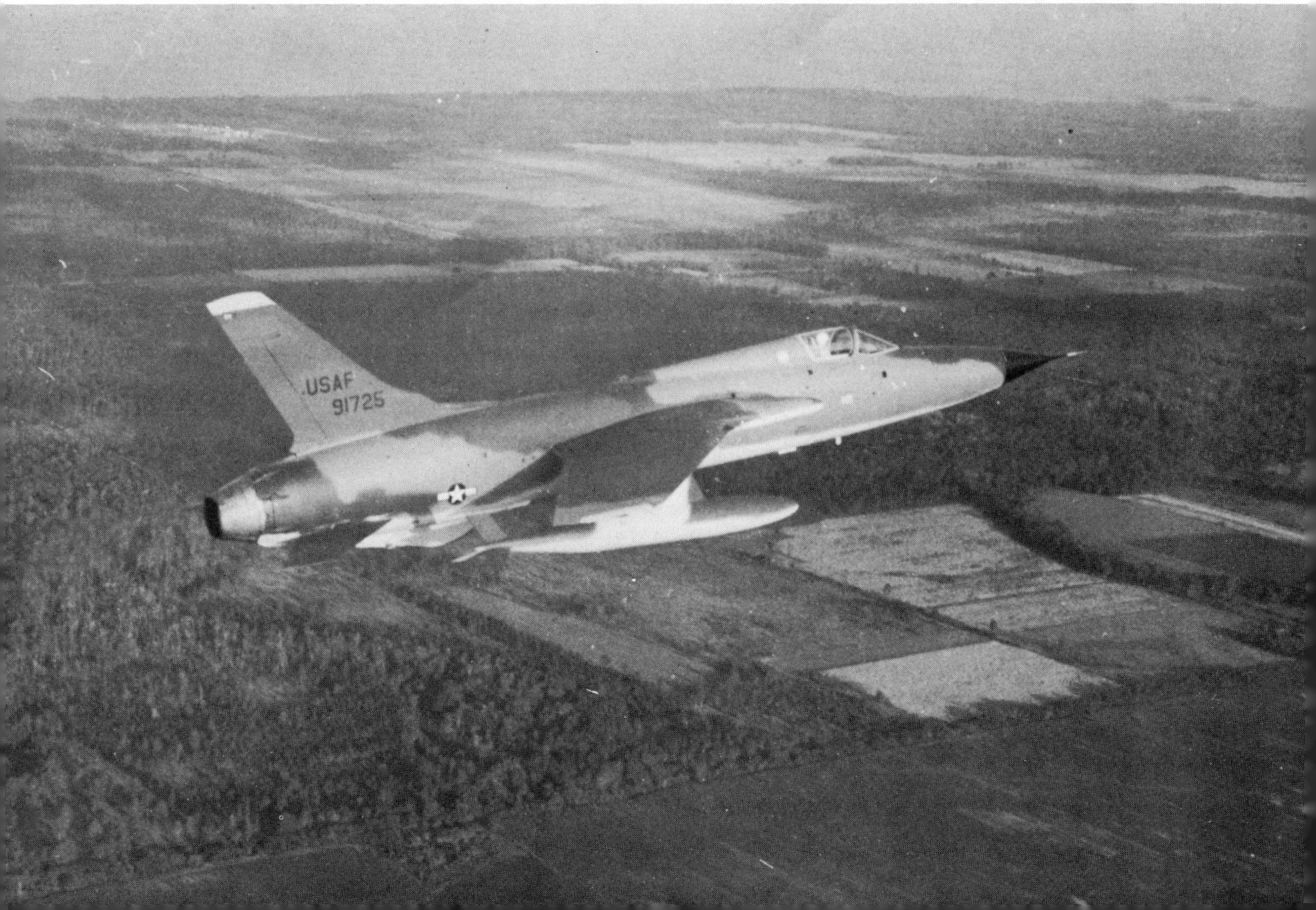

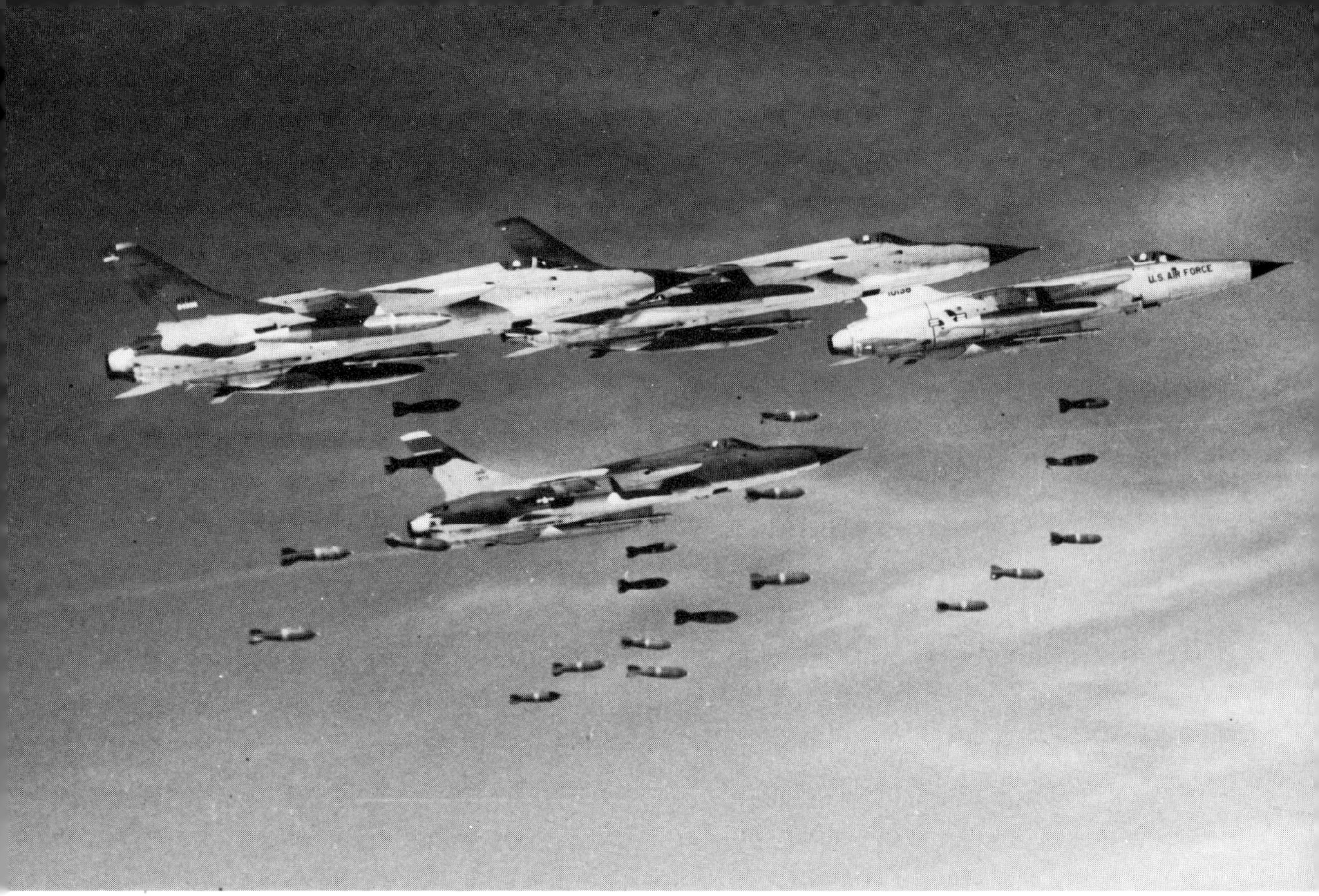

▲25 ▼26

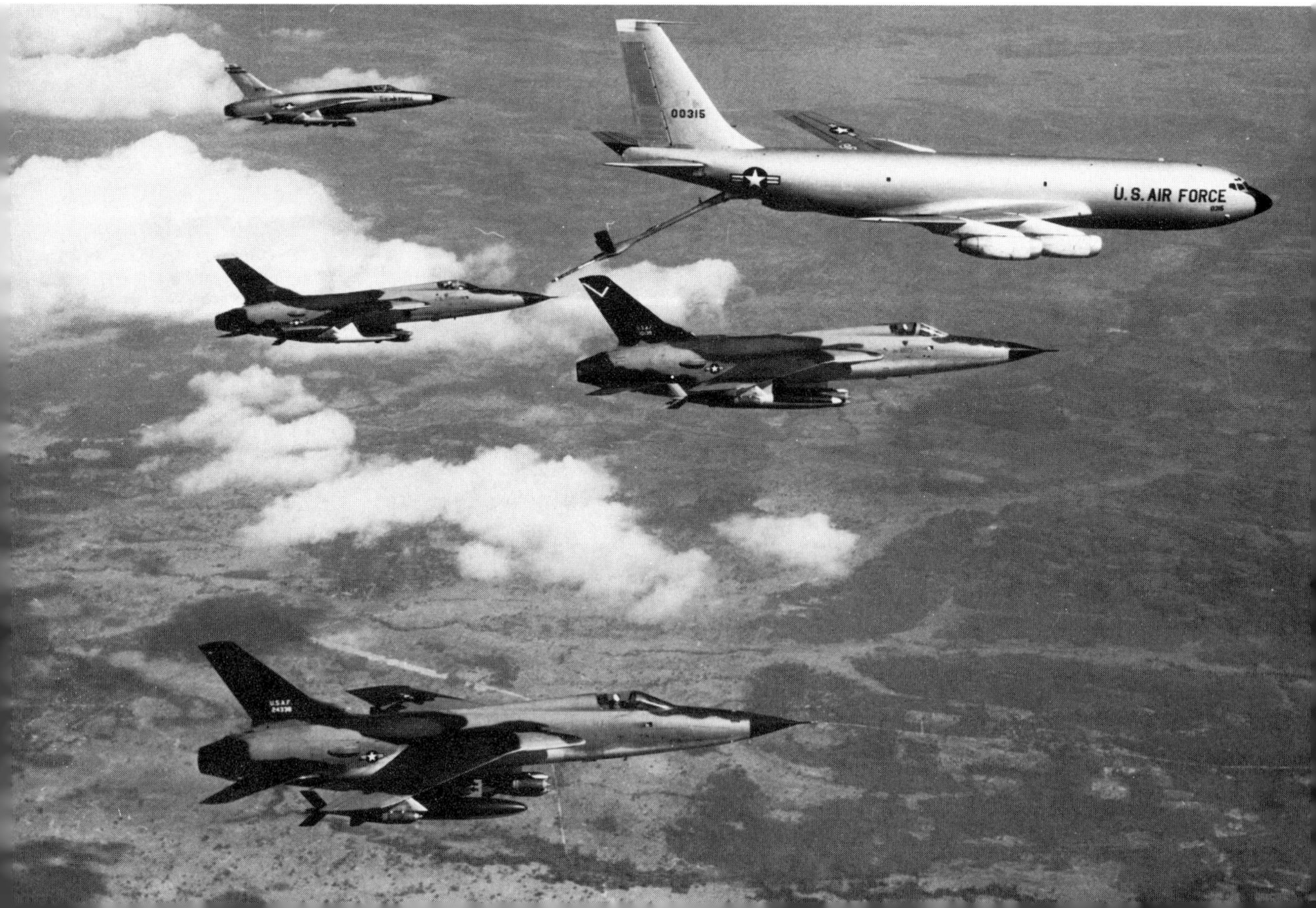

25. Taken at the moment of bomb-release on an early 'Rolling Thunder' mission over North Vietnam in 1965, this spectacular view shows the various marking schemes which appeared on Thunderchiefs before two-letter tail codes came along. The flight leader is in natural aluminium finish; the two aircraft in the foreground have standard, Vietnam-era T.O. 1-1-4 camouflage; and the machine in the background has the same camouflage scheme, but with the colour pattern reversed. (Republic)

26. F-105D Thunderchiefs of the 18th TFW taking on fuel from a KC-135A tanker in South-East Asia in 1966. By mid to late 1965, the natural aluminium finish seen on the aircraft at upper left had given way to T.O. 1-1-4 camouflage as worn by the other 'Thuds'.

(Via Marty J. Isham)

27. Two-letter tactical unit identifiers, or tail codes, began to appear on camouflaged aircraft in late 1965. Here an 'RM'-coded F-105D Thunderchief of the 333rd TFS/355th TFW heads from Takhli on a combat mission, its camouflaged tail catching a glint of sunlight. (Republic)

28. Passing through Hickam AB, Hawaii, in 1968 *en route* to combat in Vietnam, two F-105Fs (63-8319 and 63-8351) make a rapid take-off. The F-model was used by a unit called 'Ryan's Raiders' on night and bad-weather missions over North Vietnam. (Nicholas M. Williams)

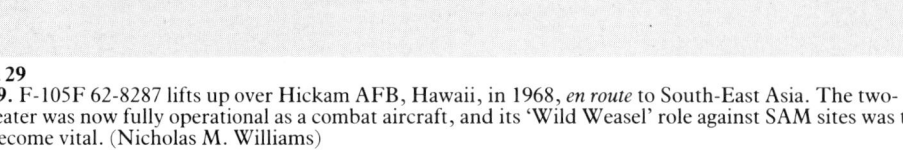

▲ 29

29. F-105F 62-8287 lifts up over Hickam AFB, Hawaii, in 1968, *en route* to South-East Asia. The two-seater was now fully operational as a combat aircraft, and its 'Wild Weasel' role against SAM sites was to become vital. (Nicholas M. Williams)

30. When camouflage appeared, it seemed to make the 'Thud' look rather drab, at least before the introduction of tail codes. This F-105D, 60-0461, is flying over the bombing range near Nellis AFB in about 1968, with empty centreline and wing ordnance stations. (USAF)

31. Stateside crews trained on the 'Thud' with the 23rd TFW at McConnell AFB, Kansas, where South-East Asia-style camouflage was adopted in the late 1960s. In this photograph F-105F 63-8303 sits beside F-105D 61-0044 on the McConnell ramp. (Via Marty J. Isham)

32. Statistically, it was 'impossible' for a 'Thud' pilot to complete 100 combat missions over North Vietnam and come out alive – and many did not. When the magic '100' *was* reached, as in this scene with the 388th TFW at Korat, Thailand, the surviving F-105 pilot was likely to get a thorough wetting from a fire hose as he stepped down from his cockpit or be heaved into the Korat swimming pool by his pals. (Col. Dave Roeder)

▼ 30

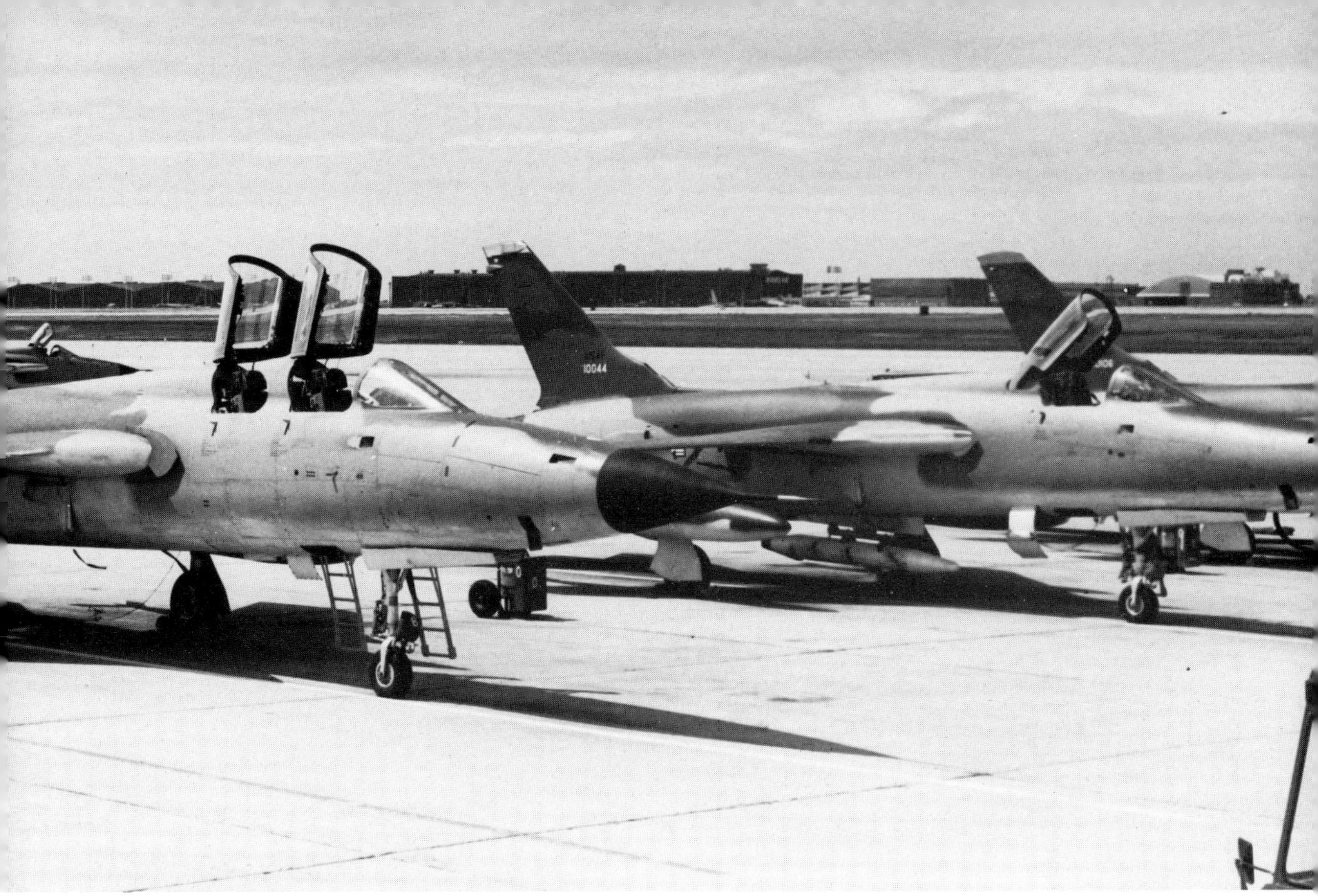

31▲ 32▼

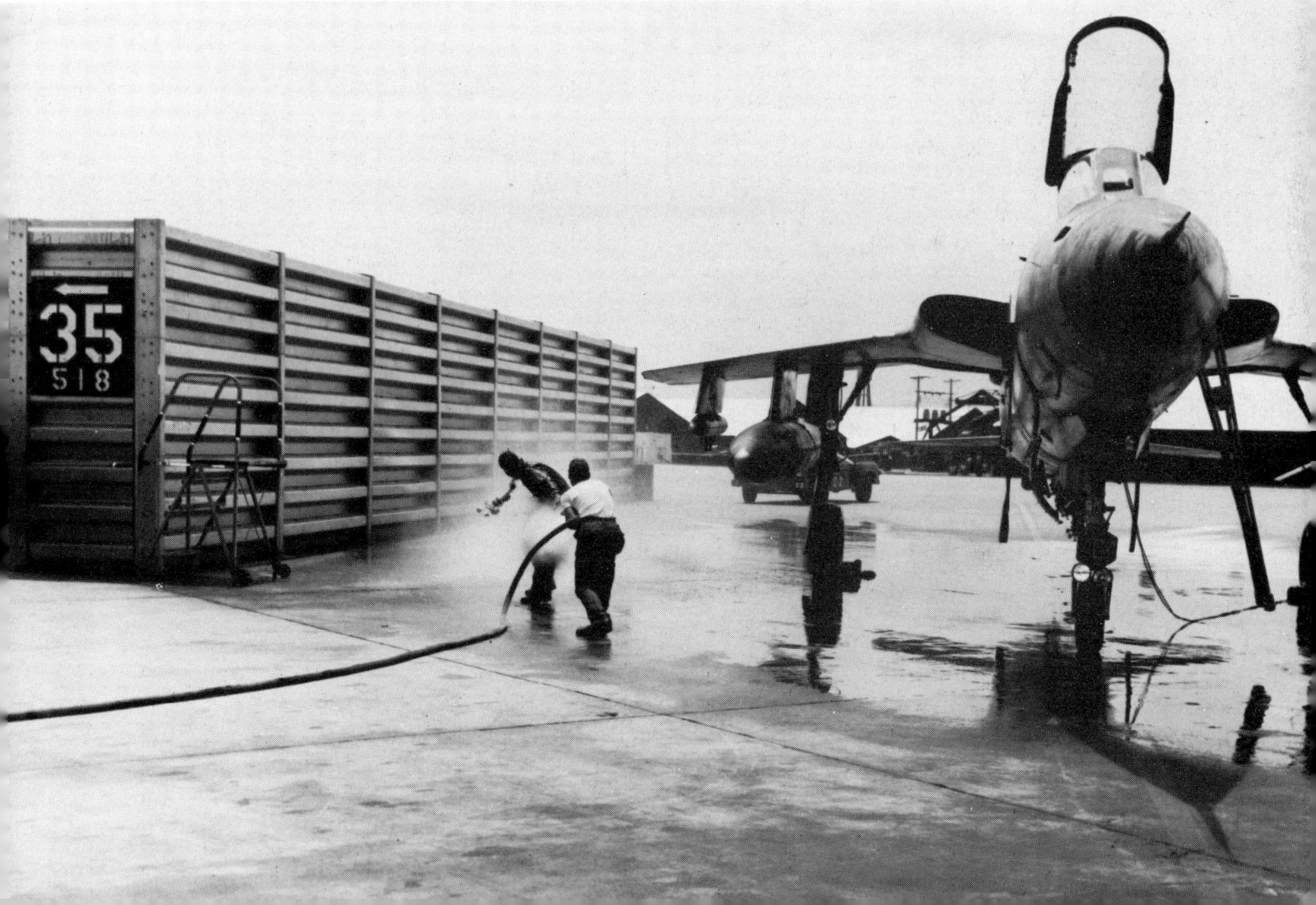

▲33   ▼34

33. F-105D 62-4405 flies beside a tanker during a 'Rolling Thunder' mission against North Vietnam. Its bombs create black silhouettes beneath the fuselage and outboard wing station; the other 'protrusions' below the Thunderchief are an F-4C Phantom wingman. (Col. Harry Wilson)

34. Although they never reached the combat zone, B-model Thunderchiefs were also painted in South-East Asia camouflage. F-105B 57-5820 has just received the new scheme and is ready for delivery to an Air National Guard (ANG) unit. (Via Marty J.Isham)

35. F-105F 62-4424 of the 36th TFW, at Soesterberg, Holland. (USAF)

▲ 36

▲ 37   ▼ 38

36. F-105F 62-4423 at Andrews AFB, Maryland, in the mid-1960s. (Roger F. Besecker)

37. 'RE' is the code for F-105F 63-8302, 44th TFS/355th TFW, based at Takhli, Thailand. This F-model has the nickname 'Half a Yard' painted on a black field along the air intakes and was flown by Lt. Col. Ed Moriarty. (Donald L. Jay)

38. 'Big Sal' was the nickname inscribed in a black surround on the intake of F-105D 61-0086. This Thunderchief, from the 44th TFS/355th TFW based at Takhli in Thailand, wears the 'RE' tail code and is seen heading north carrying external fuel and bombs with extender fuses. (Via Marty J. Isham)

39. The unsung F-105 heroes were the maintenance crews who struggled in the Thai heat to keep the 'Thuds' flying, often working all night to prepare a morning mission. Here mechanics and armourers work on the 20mm M61A1 cannon of an F-105D, 16 November 1967. (Via Eric Renth)

39▶

▲ 40

▲ 41   ▼ 42

43▲

40. *En route* to Bitburg AB, Germany, two F-105D Thunderchiefs (60-0482 is in the foreground) suck up fuel from a brightly painted KB-50J Superfortress tanker. These 'One-Oh-Fives' belong to the 23rd TFS/36th TFW and are in natural aluminum finish. (Donald L. Jay)

41. F-105B 57-5814 in *Thunderbirds* markings flies in formation with a civil-registered F8F Bearcat. (Via Marty J. Isham)

42, 43. F-105D Thunderchiefs of the 354th TFS/355th TFW aloft in April 1965. The previous month, President Johnson had instituted the 'Rolling Thunder' campaign against North Vietnam. Throughout 1965–68 'Thuds' carried the heaviest burden in South-East Asia. (D. Steigers)

44. A close-up view of the AGM-45A Shrike anti-radiation missile (ARM), employed with success against North Vietnamese SAM sites by F-105F and F-105G Wild Weasels. Shrike was 10ft in length, with a body diameter of 8in and a span of 36in. (Donald L. Jay)

44▼

▲45

45. The 'Thud' went off to what seemed, at first, a small and romantic war, wearing its aluminium-coating finish and brandishing shark's teeth. Here F-105D 61-0163 of the 23rd Tactical Fighter Wing carries bombs over South-East Asia, 1965. (Harrison D. Rued)

46. Introduced on the F-105G variant and considered more advanced than the Shrike, the AGM-78 Standard ARM missile was also used against SA-2 'Guideline' missile installations. Standard ARM was 15ft long, had a body diameter of 1ft 1½in and had a

rear-fin span of 3ft 7in. (Donald L. Jay)

47. F-105F Wild Weasel 'Half A Yard', aircraft 63-8302, of the 44th TFS/355th TFW, bores through South-East Asian skies in April 1970. (Donald L. Jay)

48. Typical of the nicknames affixed to 'Thuds' in combat was 'Arkansas Traveler', the F-105D flown by Col. Paul P. Douglas Jr., commander of the 388th TFW at Korat. Douglas, a Second World War ace, had previously had the name on his P-47 Thunderbolt. (USAF)

▼46

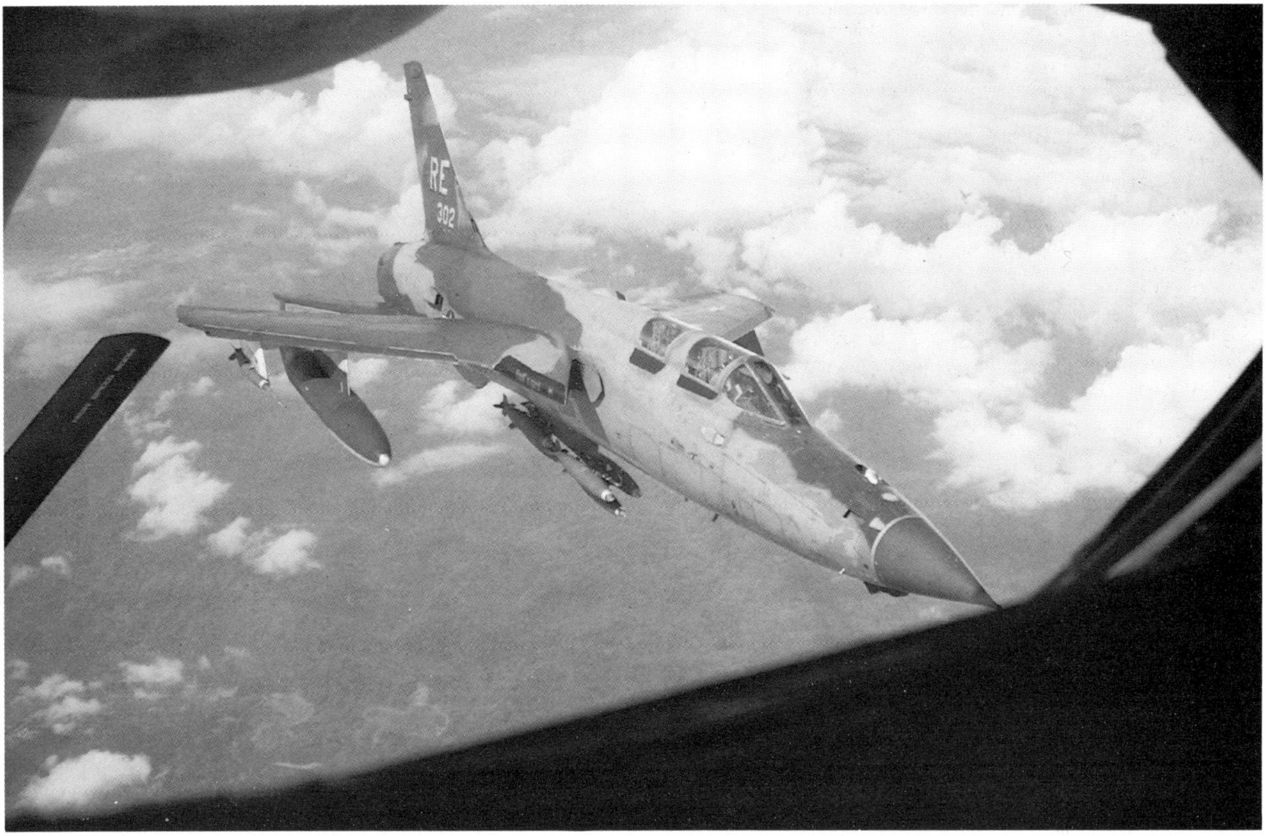
RE
302

47▲ 48▼

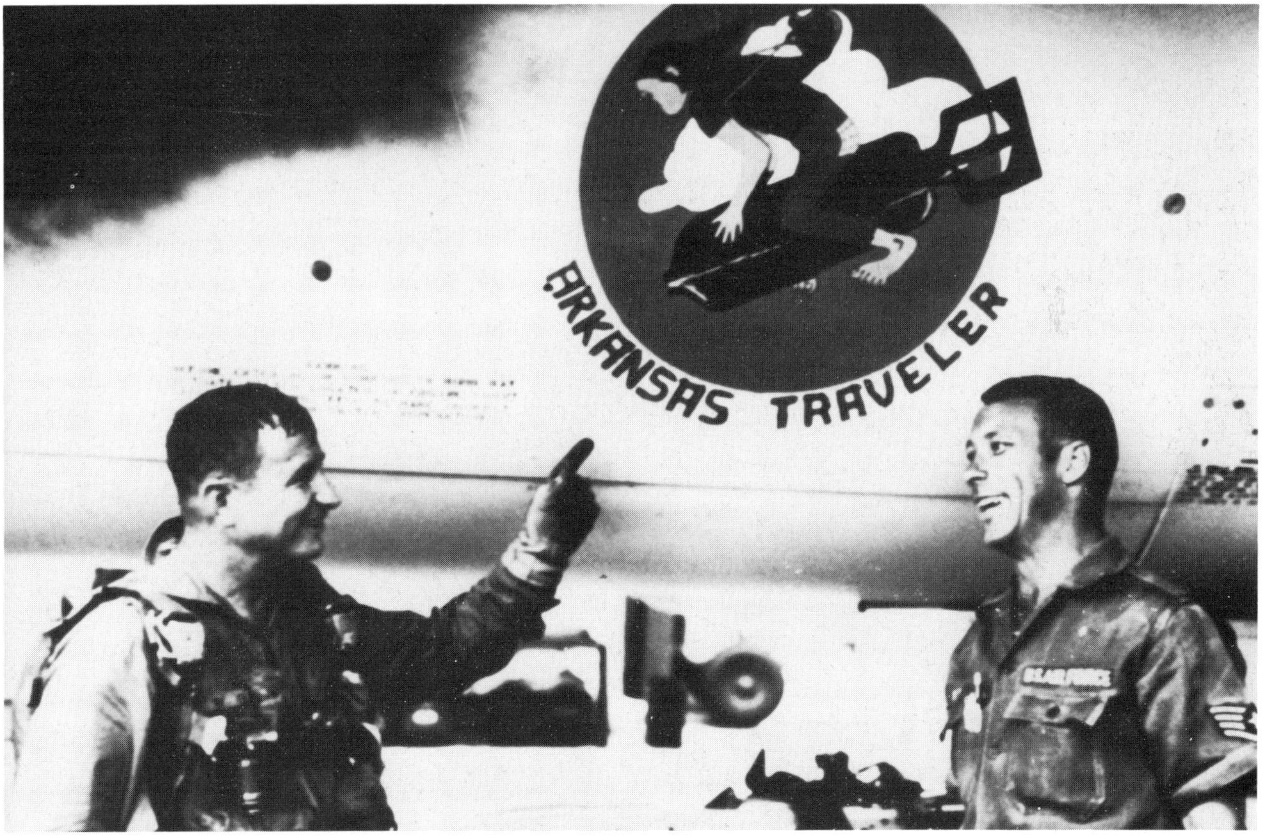
ARKANSAS TRAVELER
U.S. AIR FORCE

49. F-105D 62-4284 was the champion MiG-killer among 'Thuds'. Capt. Max C. Brestel shot down two MiG-17s while flying this aircraft with the call-sign 'Kangaroo Four' on 10 March 1967, and Capt. Gene I. Basel despatched a third MiG-17 on 27 October 1967. Seen here with centreline bombs and outboard cluster bomb units (CBUs), '284 belonged to the 354th TFS/355th TFW at Takhli. (Donald L. Jay)

50. Illustrating how T.O. 1-1-4 camouflage can blend in with the jungle, F-105D 59-1771 speeds along at low altitude. With its 'JV' tail code, the aircraft belongs to the 469th TFS/388th TFW stationed at Takhli. Low-level flying was a regular challenge for 'Thud' pilots. (Col. Dave Roeder)

51. A Kaman HH-43B 'Pedro' equipped for air-base fire-fighting hovers over F-105 Thunderchiefs at Korat. The aircraft on the far left is an F-105F Wild Weasel carrying AGM-45 Shrike missiles for strikes against surface-to-air (SAM) missile sites. (Via Eric Renth)

49▶

▼50

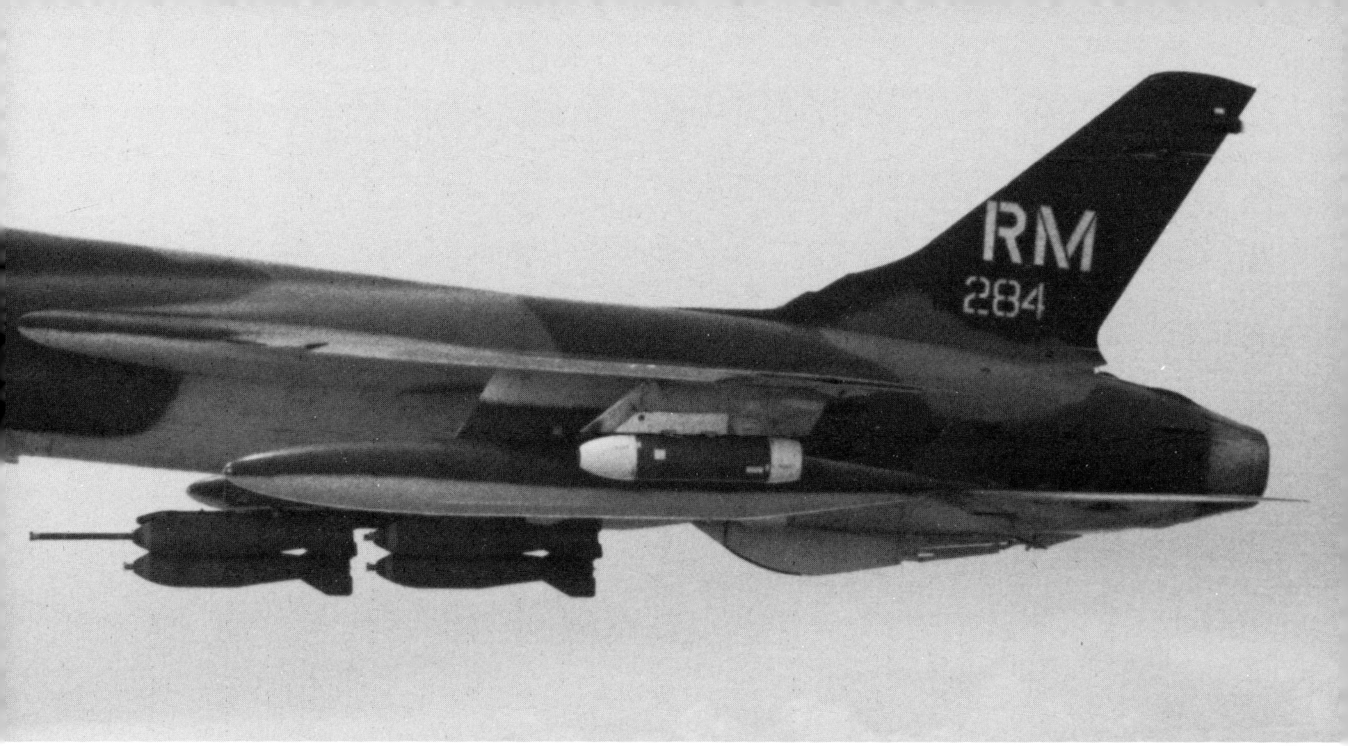

51▼

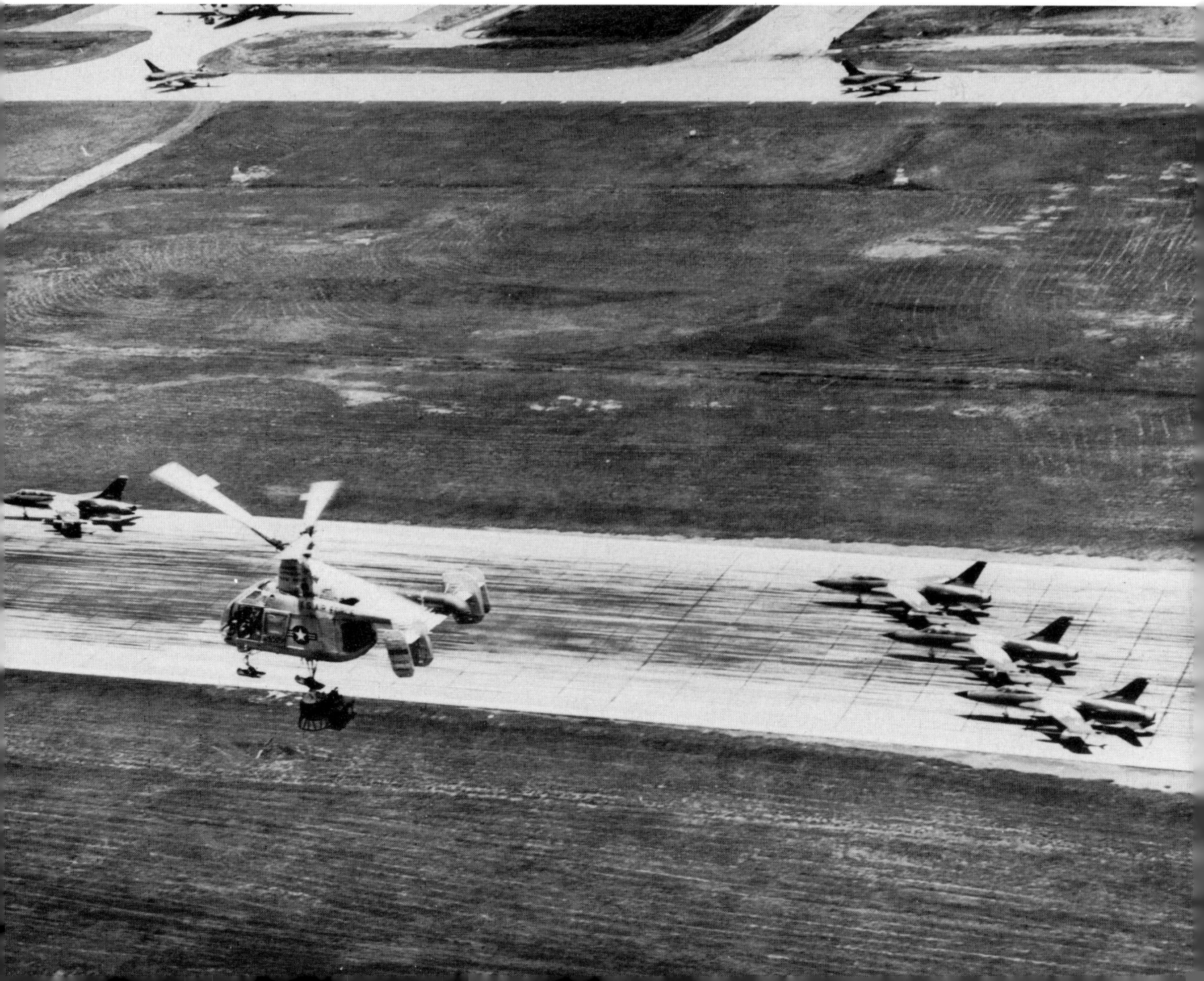

▲ 52

▲ 53   ▼ 54

52. A Wild Weasel mission, for which F-105D 62-4367 of the 333rd TFS/355th TFW (foreground) is armed with AGM-12B Bullpup air-to-surface missiles and F-105F Wild Weasel 63-8311 of the 354th TFS/355th TFW carries AGM-45A Shrike anti-radiation missiles. This combination proved very potent in attacks on North Vietnam's network of SA-2 'Guideline' SAMs. (Republic)

53. An 'RK'-coded 'Thud', 59-1729 of the 333rd TFS/355th TFW, carries centreline bombs with fuse extenders, heading towards targets in North Vietnam. MiG pilots tried to ambush the 'Thud' when it was burdened with wing tanks and fuel: in 'clean' condition the F-105D could hold its own against both MiG-17s and MiG-21s. (Via Eric Renth)

54. An F-105D taking off from Takhli for a mission. (Via Eric Renth)

55. Republic F-105D 59-1739, coded 'RM', of the 354th TFS/355th TFW, not at its Takhli home base but in depot maintenance at McClellan AFB, California, in February 1970. F-105 combat operations were extensively supported at McClellan. (Donald L. Jay)

56. While the Vietnam War was raging, the 1968 *Pueblo* incident threatened another conflict in North-East Asia. F-105D 61-0093, coded 'GR' and assigned to the 80th TFS/347th TFW at Misawa AB in Japan, was typical of the 'Thuds' committed to defending Korea. (Nagata via Marty J. Isham)

57. While F-105D and F-105F fighters waged war in South-East Asia, the older B-models began to reach the Air National Guard. F-105B 57-5840, which was in fact the last F-105B built, went to the 141st TFS, New Jersey ANG. (Via Marty J. Isham)

55▲

56▲   57▼

▲58

▲59   ▼60

61 ▲

58. Other F-105Bs went to the Air Force Reserve, which operated them with considerable success. Aircraft 57-1816, coded 'HI', went to the 466th TFS/508th TFG at Hill AFB, Utah. (Author)
59. While the 'Thud' was still the 'hottest' thing in the skies and still challenging Hanoi's defences, one ageing F-105B became the first 'gate guardian,' or exhibit aircraft, in the series: 54-0107 is displayed outdoors, July 1970, at Lackland AFB, Texas, where all USAF basic training is conducted. (Norman Taylor)
60. The two-seat F-105F, used with stealth, vigour and determination against Hanoi's missile sites, was in fact designated EF-105F, although the men who flew and maintained the aircraft never used the term. This example, 63-8327, coded 'JE', belonged

to the 44th TFS at Korat. (Col. Dave Roeder)
61. Wearing the natural metal exterior which went out of fashion at most places, F-105F Wild Weasel 62-4419 is seen at China Lake, California, on 27 May 1965. The AGM-45 Shrike anti-radiation missile on the outboard wing station was being tested in the California desert. (Via Marty J. Isham)
62. Development of the two-seat Wild Weasel aircraft continued in a variety of locations even after President Johnson halted the bombing of North Vietnam on 31 October 1968. Here F-105F (or EF-105F) 62-4438 of the 66th Fighter Weapons Squadron, coded 'WC', flies over Nellis AFB, Nevada. (Via Marty J. Isham)

62 ▼

▲63

63. The 35th Tactical Fighter Wing at George AFB, California, kept 'Thud' combat crews up to standard during and after the Vietnam conflict. This F-105G Wild Weasel, 63-8307, demonstrates the QRC-380 blisters on the lower fuselage beneath the wing. (Via Marty J. Isham)

64. With the success of the Wild Weasel, the decision was made to develop the F-105G model, which was an F-105F equipped with QRC-380 blisters on either side of its fuselage, housing electronics gear used to pin-point SAM sites. The F-105G also introduced the capability to use the AGM-78 Standard ARM missile. Seen here on 5 May 1970, aircraft 62-4434 tested the F-105G concept at Eglin AFB, Florida. It carries two AGM-78B Standard ARM missiles as well as two AGM-45 Shrikes. (Via Marty J. Isham)

65. F-105F Thunderchiefs of the 66th Fighter Weapons Squadron at Nellis AFB, Nevada; 63-8266 is in the foreground. The South-East Asia camouflage scheme included light undersides, although 'Ryan's Raiders' in Vietnam had employed 'wraparound' camouflage as early as 1966. (Via Marty J. Isham)

64 ▲   65 ▼

▲ 66   ▼ 67

68 ▲

69 ▲

66. In the combat zone, Weasels operated in flights of four, sometimes with an all-F-105F (or F-105G) composition, sometimes with two F-105D single-seaters included in the formation. In this photograph, taken in the USA, four F-105G Wild Weasels of the 35th TFW fly together. (Via Marty J. Isham)

67. F-105D 60-0525 ready for inspection at Nellis with the pilot at parade rest. The 'Thud' has a full bomb load, and its refuelling probe is extended. The sign beside the pilot says that the F-105 has a speed of 1,380mph, a ceiling of 52,000ft and a range of 2,012 miles. (Via Marty J. Isham)

68. Not often pictured is the 12th TFS/18th TRF, which was stationed at Kadena AB, Okinawa, during the Vietnam conflict. F-105F two-seater 63-8268 wears standard camouflage, plus the yellow canopy rails and ring around the nose which were unique to this unit. (Nagata via Marty J. Isham)

69. F-105D 60-0529 in flight over South-East Asia with six 750lb bombs. (Via Marty J. Isham)

70. Devoid of ordnance or missiles, F-105D 61-0161 of the 44th TFS/355th TFW wings through South-East Asian skies near Takhli on 30 October 1969. The 'Thud' is returning from a mission, its payload spent and its fuel low. (Via Marty J. Isham)

70 ▼

▲71

71. F-105F Thunderchief 62-4424 of the 388th TFW from Korat heads into action carrying 750lb bombs. Barely perceptible beneath the wing root is 'Seagram's 7', the aircraft's nickname, after a well-known brand of whisky. (Donald L. Jay)

72. Two F-105D Thunderchiefs follow an F-100D Super Sabre on a mission. The 'Thud' in the background has a reverse camouflage pattern, although with the colours correct. (Via Marty J. Isham)

73. F-105Ds and F-105Fs fought courageously in the 1965–68 'Rolling Thunder' campaign against North Vietnam but soon afterwards began to be replaced by F-4 Phantoms. The F-105G

Wild Weasel fought in the second major campaign over North Vietnam, called 'Linebacker', which lasted from 8 May 1972 until the 27 January 1973 cease-fire. The 17th Wild Weasel Squadron stayed on, this F-105G (63-8291) being depicted at Korat in August 1973. (Donald L. Jay)

74. It took dozens of men, from electronics technicians to maintenance experts, to keep an F-105 Thunderchief in combat. Members of the 469th TFS/388th TFW at Korat posed for this portrait towards the end of the 1965–68 campaign, pilots on the wing and enlisted troops in the foreground. (Via Col. Dave Roeder)

▼72

73▲   74▼

▲ 75

75. The same D-models which fought in Vietnam soon became the backbone of the Air National Guard; only New Jersey flew the F-105B, but the F-105D went to several units. In this photograph, aircraft 60-0445 of the 113th TFW, District of Columbia ANG, warms up at Andrews AFB, Maryland, on 4 October 1975. (Peter B. Mersky)

76. Aircraft 60-0445 banks over countryside a few miles from Washington, DC. The DC ANG flew the D-model 'Thud' for a decade before converting to the F-4D Phantom in the mid-1980s. Note the position of the 'petals' on the exhaust nozzle, open for low-speed flight. (Peter B. Mersky)

▼ 76

77. Viewed from the front, the 'Thud' was always an awesome sight, nearly as large as a B-17 Flying Fortress. F-105D 61-0175 of the 127th TFTS, Kansas ANG, is seen here at McConnell AFB, Kansas, on 2 October 1971. (Clyde Gerdes)

78. F-105D Thunderchief 61-0086 of the 192nd TFG, Virginia ANG, wears a protective shroud over part of its nose while basking in the sun at Sandston Airport, Richmond, Virginia, in 1975. The aircraft is in standard T.O. 1-1-4 Vietnam-era camouflage, with a yellow fin flash and a small Confederate flag under the cockpit. (Roger F. Besecker)

77▲   78▼

▲ 79

▲ 80   ▼ 81

79. F-105D 58-1155 of the 113th TFW, DC ANG, at Andrews AFB on 19 March 1977. The T.O. 1-1-4 camouflage gave a plain appearance, but the aircraft had a squadron emblem below the cockpit, the ANG badge and the words 'District of Columbia' on the tail. (Author)

80. The F-105D also went to the Air Force Reserve. Here wearing black codes and the 'wraparound' camouflage which replaced light-coloured undersides in the 1980s, F-105D 62-4301 of 466th TFS/419th TFW AFRES departs from its home station at Hill AFB, Utah, in October 1983. The nickname 'My Karma' is just visible on the nose. (Douglas R. Tachauer)

81. With the designation JF-105D to indicate changes for test purposes, aircraft 59-1774 was flown at the Tactical Air Warfare Center (TAWC), Eglin AFB, Florida, as signified by the red blaze on the tail. In this photograph the aircraft is visiting Andrews AFB, 29 March 1968. (Joseph G. Handelman, DDS)

82. A bomb-laden F-105D Thunderchief, 60-0464 of the 469th TFS/388th TFW from Korat, Thailand, formates on a KC-135 tanker while *en route* to targets in North Vietnam in September 1968. A month later, President Johnson called a bombing halt, ending the 'Thud's long and gruelling campaign. (Donald L. Jay)

83. Aircraft 61-0161, with ECM pods on the outboard wing stations and a centreline bomb-load, heads towards Hanoi in September 1968. This 'JV'-coded 'Thud' belongs to the 469th TFS/388th TFW at Korat. (Donald L. Jay)

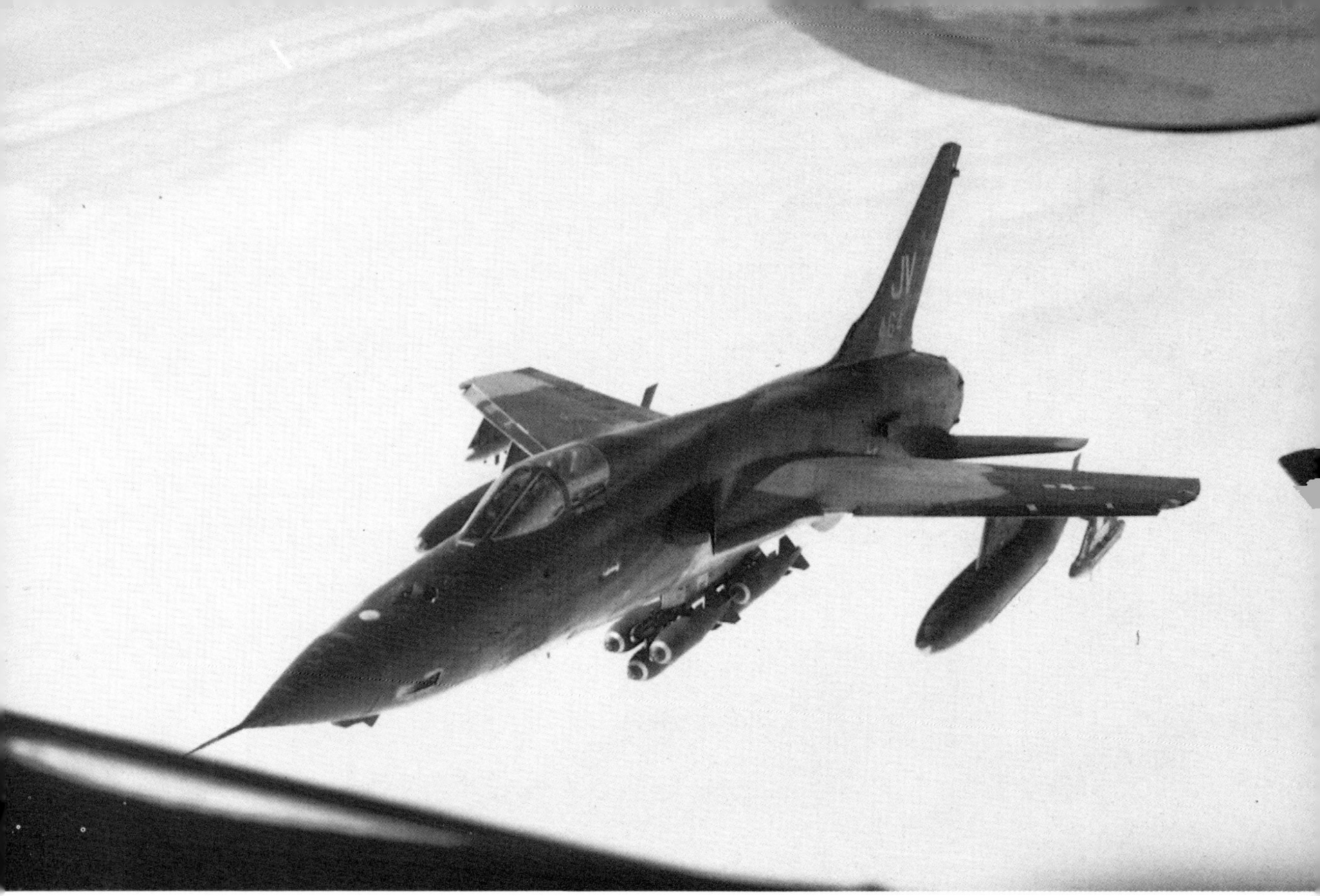

82▲ 83▼

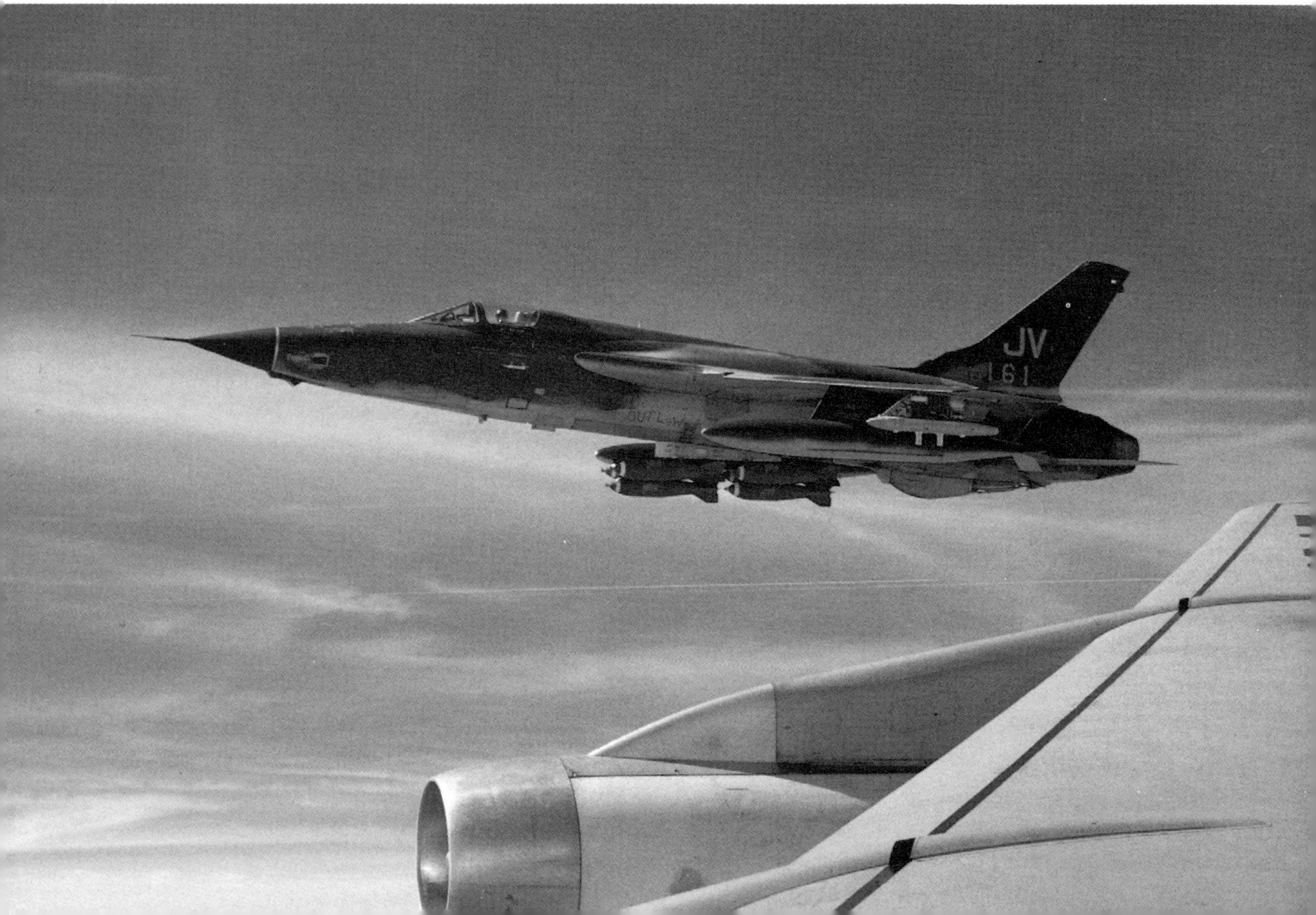

▲ 84   ▼ 85

86 ▲

84. The F-105G Wild Weasel continued to serve in the Air Guard and acquired 'wraparound' camouflage and black insignia in the 1980s. Aircraft 63-8265, with the 128th TFS/116th TFW, Georgia ANG, wears shark's teeth as well, at Dobbins AFB, Georgia, 20 August 1982. (Douglas R. Tachauer)

85. F-105Ds of the 466th TFS/308th TFW, Air Force Reserve, with 62-4361 in foreground, head out from Hill AFB, Utah, on 28 September 1983. Black tail codes were introduced in the 1980s but were not immediately followed by black national insignia. (Lindsay T. Peacock)

86. F-105G Wild Weasel 63-8306 of the 128th TFS/116th TFW at Dobbins AFB, Georgia, on 20 August 1982. (Douglas R. Tachauer)

87. F-105F 63-8299 of the 121st TFS/113rd TFW, DC ANG, at Andrews AFB on 11 November 1976. This machine later served with the Georgia ANG where, on 25 May 1983, it became the very last Thunderchief to fly. (Author)

87 ▼

▲ 88   ▼ 89

88. F-105 62-4301,
nicknamed 'My Karma' and
assigned to the 466th TFS/
508th TFG, Air Force Reserve,
was the only Thunderchief ever
to be painted in the lizard-green
'European One' camouflage
which was to become
widespread in the mid-1980s.
The colour is much denser than
the T.O. 1-1-4 Vietnam-era
camouflage. The aircraft was
photographed during a visit to
Canada. (Donald L. Jay)
89. F-105D 62-4301 'My
Karma' makes a low-level pass
over Hill AFB, Utah, in
October 1983. (Douglas R.
Tachauer)
90. The 'ME' tail code
represented the 563rd TFS/
23rd TFW at McConnell AFB,
Kansas; aircraft 61-0099,
an F-105D, is seen on a visit to
neighbouring Forbes AFB,
Kansas, on 3 October 1971.
The Tactical Air Command
badge appears above the tail
code. (Clyde Gerdes)
91. F-105D 61-0146 of the
466th TFS/301st TFW at Hill
AFB, Utah, in the early 1980s.
(Via Marty J. Isham)

90 ▲   91 ▼

▲ 92

92. Thirty F-105D aircraft were converted by July 1971 in the long-delayed 'Thunderstick II' programme, which placed new avionics in a dorsal fairing behind the pilot. Aircraft 60-0471 served with the 457th TFS/301st TFW, Air Force Reserve, but was in storage in New Mexico by the time it was photographed in April 1983. This aircraft was one of several used for battle damage repair training.

▼ 93

(Philip A. Tachauer)

93. Viewed from close-up, the skin of the Thunderchief's fuselage was a hodge-podge of metal plates and protrusions, including a strike camera retrofit just below the radome. F-105D 58-1155 of the DC ANG is seen at Andrews AFB, Maryland, on 19 March 1977. (Author)

94 ▲

94. An F-105F of the 128th TFS/116th TFW, Georgia ANG, takes off from Dobbins AFB in May 1983. This unit employed both F- and G-model two-seaters. The aircraft still has Vietnam-era camouflage, with the state name in a black-bordered yellow band on the tail. (Don Spering/AIR)
95. An F-105G of the Georgia ANG aloft in February 1982. Note the QRC-380 blisters on the lower fuselage, beneath the wings, which denote a G-model. Equipped with wing tanks, multiple ejector racks (MER) with Mk. 76 practice bombs and AGM-45 dummy Shrikes on the wing pylons, the aircraft is heading for the Pinecastle range in Florida. (Don Spering/AIR)

95 ▼

96. F-105D 60-0449 of the 192nd TFG, Virginia Air National Guard, at Byrd Field near Richmond in 1975. The Virginia unit eventually converted from the mighty 'Thud' to the Vought A-7D Corsair II. (Roger F. Besecker)

97. One of the more unusual paint schemes to appear on a Thunderchief was that for the bicentennial year of American independence in 1976, when New Jersey ANG's F-105B 57-5776 received a light blue tail with a Minuteman emblem and red and white rudder stripes. This photograph was taken at McGuire AFB, New Jersey, on 31 May 1976. (Clyde Gerdes)

98. By the early 1980s, Thunderchief 'gate guardians' began to appear in several locations. Aircraft 54-100, the very first F-105B, was given a bogus '105' tail number and placed on a pylon at McClellan AFB, California, where much 'Thud work' had been performed. (Author)

96 ▶

▼ 97

New Jersey

57-5776

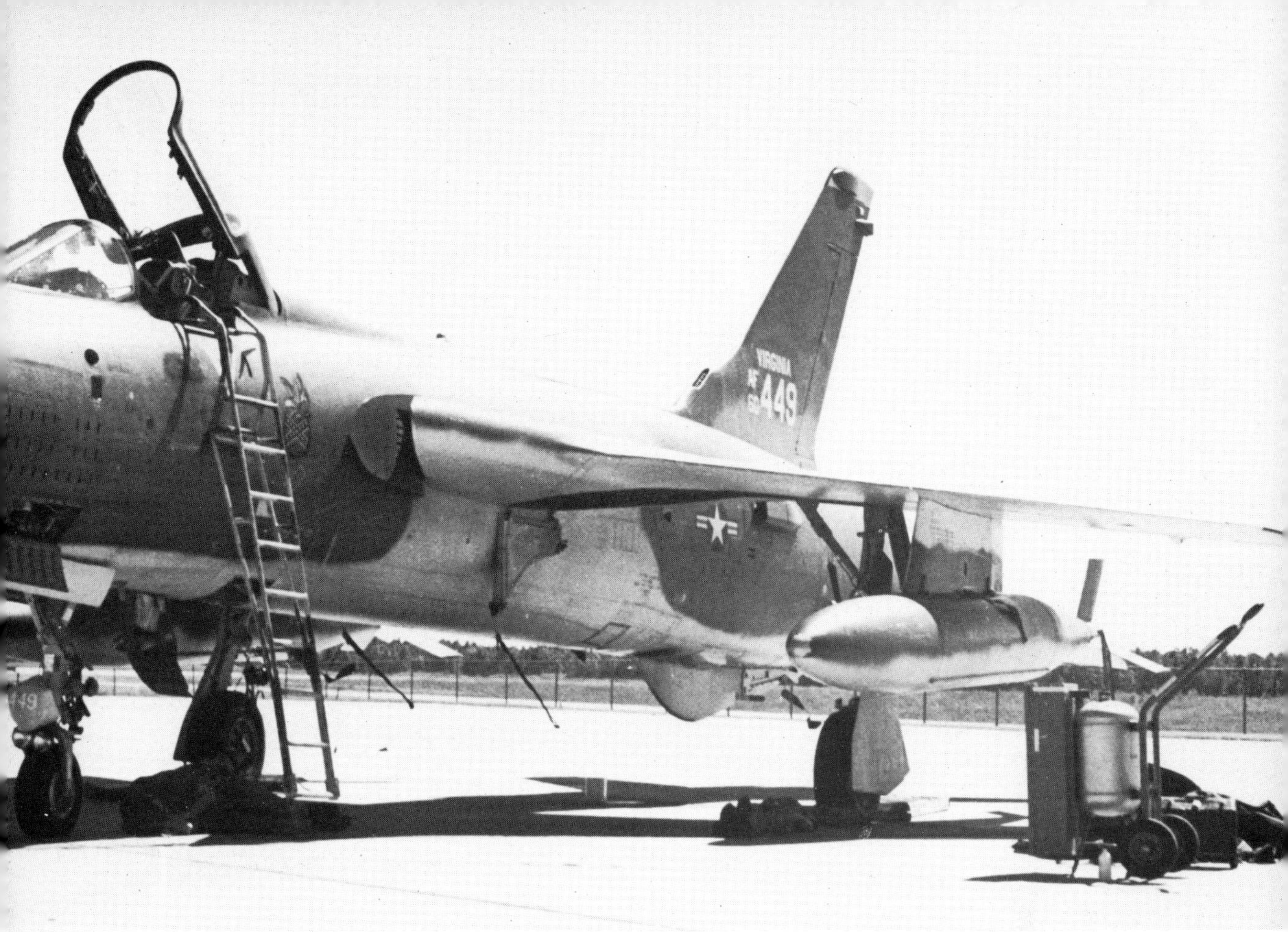

98 ▼

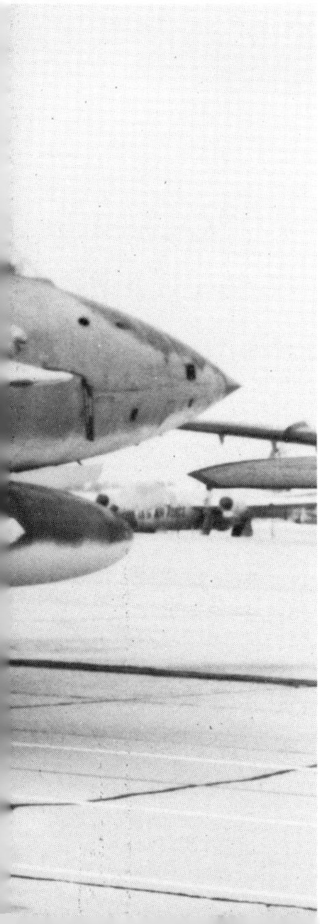

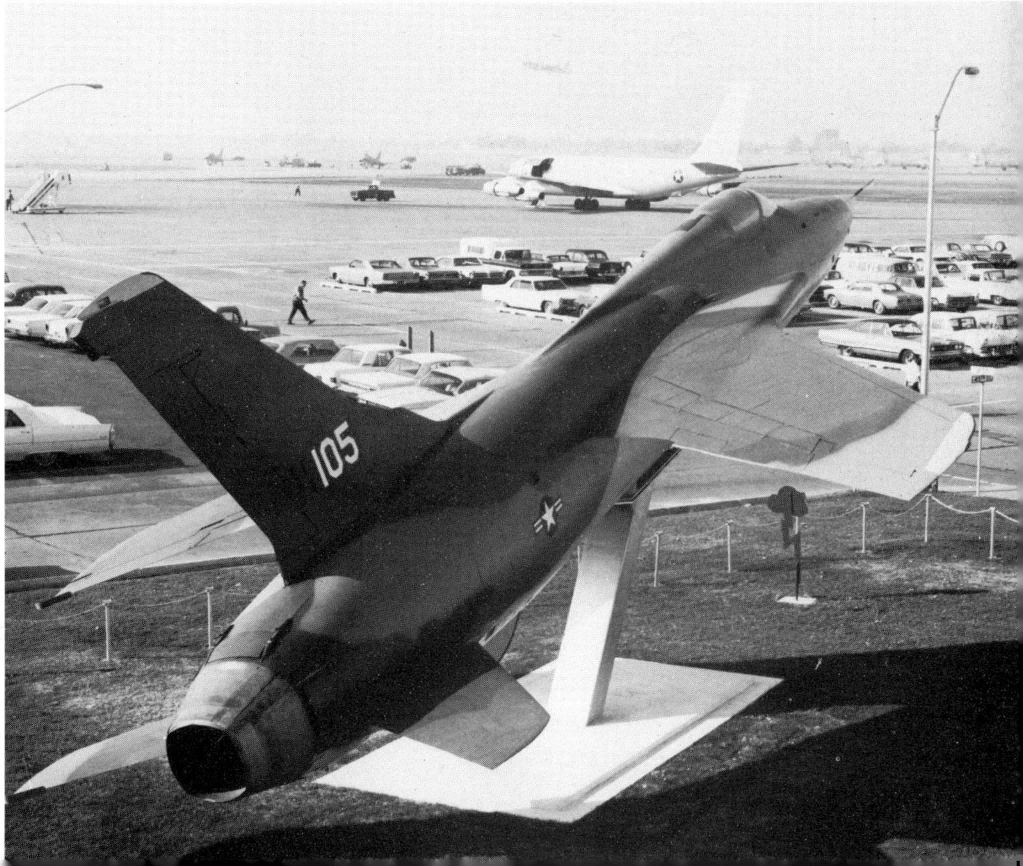

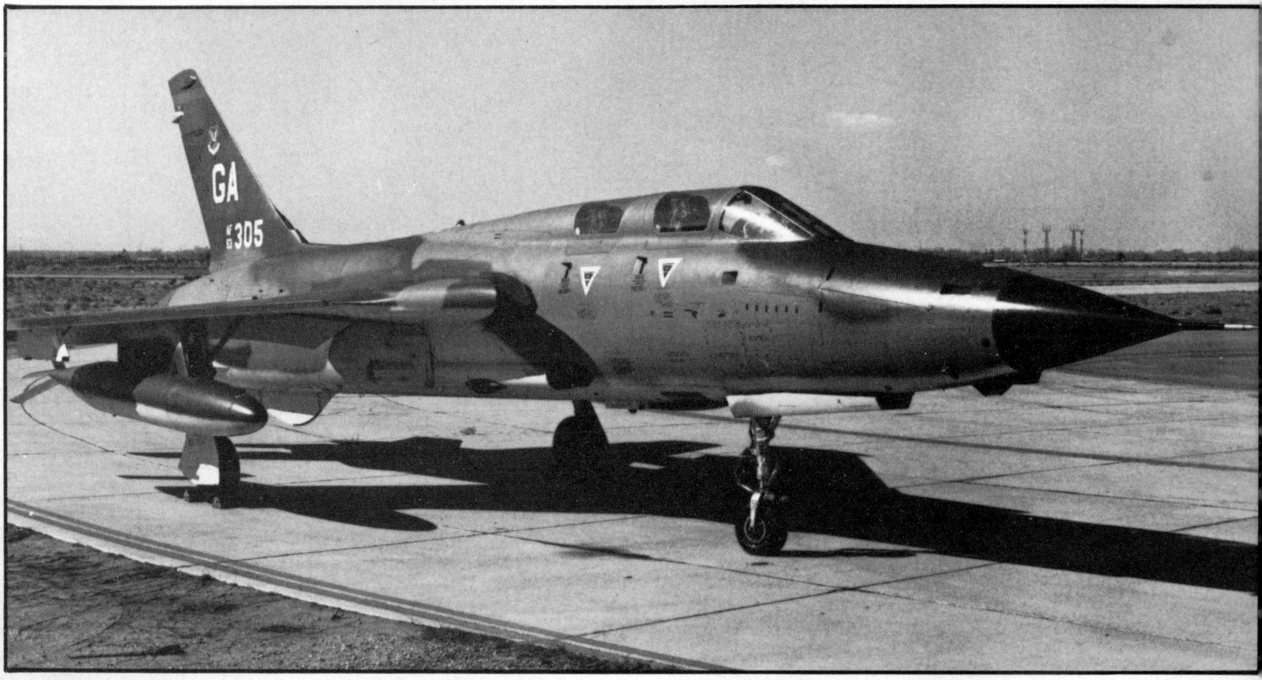
GA
AF 63 305

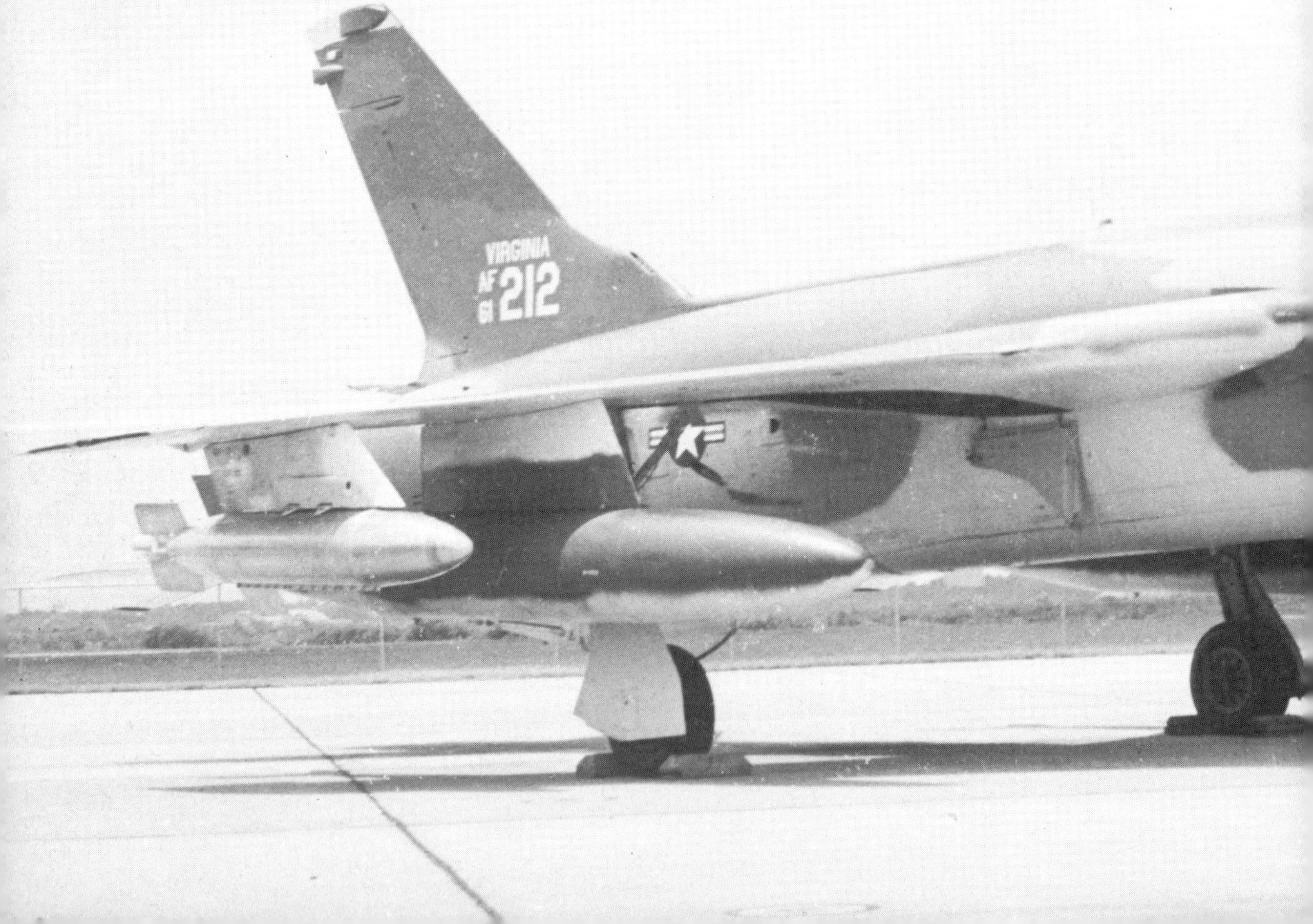
VIRGINIA
AF 61 212

◄ 99

100 ▲   101 ▼

99. One of the last active-duty Air Force units to operate the 'Thud', before it became solely an Air National Guard and Reserve machine, was the 35th TFW at George AFB, California. The Wing's F-105G Wild Weasel, 63-8305, is seen in a pristine state on the George ramp. (Via Marty J. Isham)

100. F-105D 61-0204, 127th TFTS Kansas ANG, at McConnell AFB, 2 October 1971. (Clyde Gerdes)
101. F-105D 61-0212, 149th TFS/192nd TFG, Virginia ANG, at Byrd Field near Richmond in 1975. (Clyde Gerdes)

▲102

102. F-105D Thunderchief 61-0167 of the 149th TFS/192nd TFG, Virginia ANG, at Byrd Field near Richmond in June 1974. Unlike more recent fighters, the 'Thud' did not have parachute affixed to its seat: the pilot wore the 'chute slung over his back – and it was a long climb up to the cockpit. (Jerry Geer)

103–106. Further Air National Guard F-105Ds: 62-4253, 127th TFTS, at McConnell on 2 October 1971 (photos 103, 104); 62-4291 at McConnell, 2 October 1971 (photo 105); and 64-4361 at McConnell, 2 October 1971 (photo 106). (Clyde Gerdes)

▼103

104 ▲

105 ▲   106 ▼

▲107

▲108 ▼109

107. F-105D 62-4372, wearing the 'SH' tail code of the 301st TFW, Air Force Reserve, at Carswell AFB, Texas, in about 1975. (Clyde Gerdes)

108. F-105D 62-4387 at McConnell, 2 October 1971. (Clyde Gerdes)

109. The Thunderchief may have been the biggest single-engine aircraft ever built, and it was certainly one of the strongest – witness this maintenance man standing on its wing. F-105F 62-4433, of the 121st TFS/113th TFW, DC ANG, was one of the last two-seaters in service and is seen here at Andrews AFB on 19 March 1977. (Author)

110. A 'WW' for Wild Weasel tail code finally became available just as the 'Thud' was leaving the active USAF inventory. F-105G 63-8292 displays the evocative coding (most are simply abbreviations of place names) shortly before being relegated to an ANG unit. (Donald L. Jay)

111. Another example of a 'WW'-coded 'Thud' was aircraft 62-8440, seen here at an air show in the USA. (USAF)

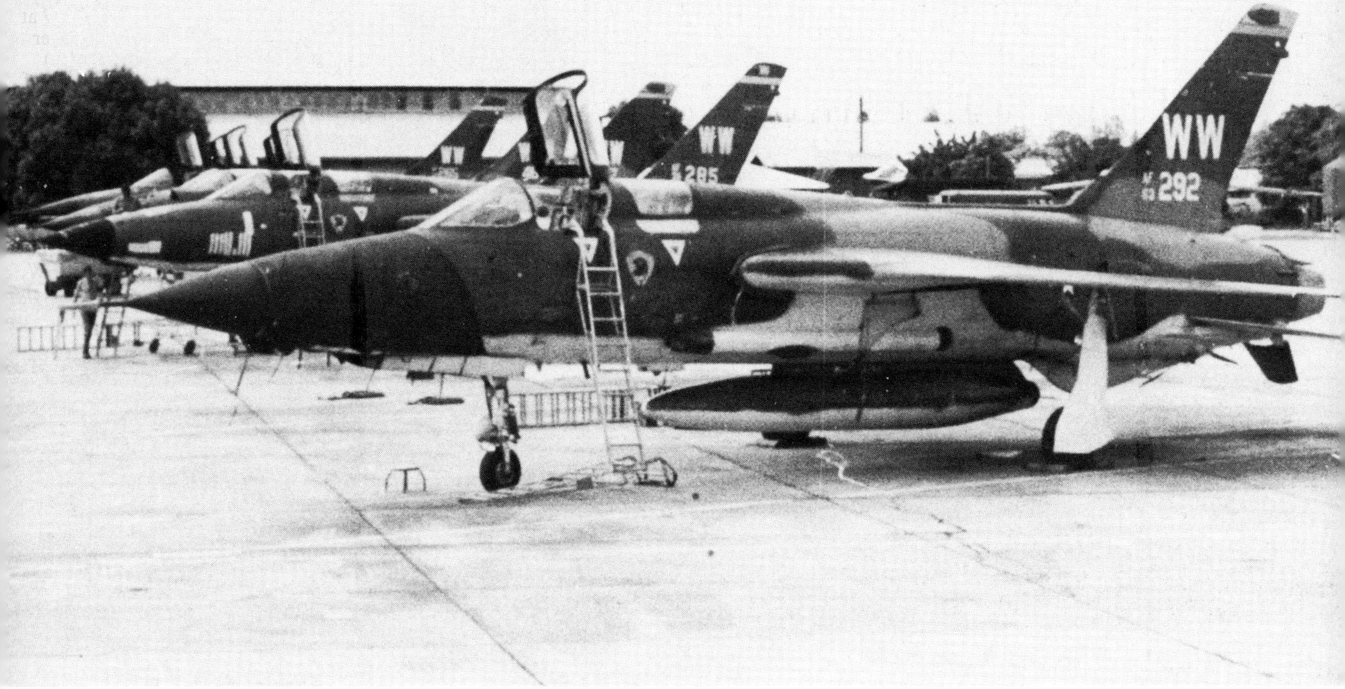

110▲ 111▼

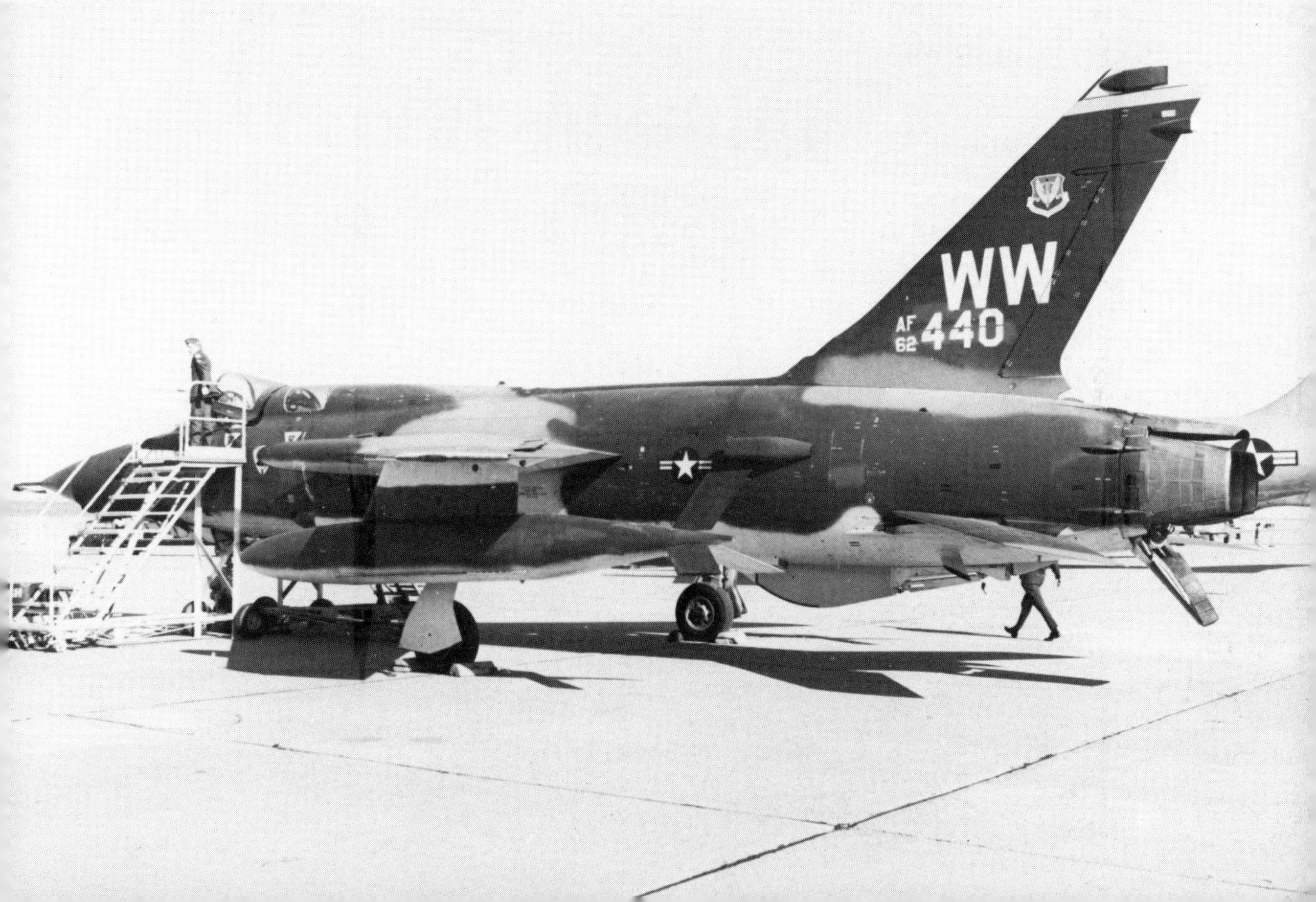

▲ 112

112. Eventually the best-preserved of Thunderchief gate guardians, the number three F-105B, 54-0102, is on display in the Battleship Memorial Park in Mobile, Alabama. Capt. W. J. Diffley, executive director for the park, says 'One of our men is an absolute genius when it comes to restoring aircraft'. The markings, including red trim in the dorsal area and on the tail, certainly appear accurate. (Eric Renth)

▼ 113

113. An F-105F of the 149th TFS/192nd TFG, Virginia Air National Guard, at Byrd Field on 6 November 1971. (Frank Hartman)

114. Before the last 'Thud' left Kansas, McConnell AFB, with at least 110 machines, had more Thunderchiefs on the base than anywhere else. Here F-105D 60-0504 poses in front of the Guard's hangar. (Kansas ANG)

▲115   ▼116

115, 116. 'Wraparound' camouflage, introduced in the 1980s, made the Thunderchief hard to see whenever it had ground in the distance. F-105D 62-4387 (photo 115) with Vietnam-era T.O. 1-1-4 camouflage including light-coloured undersurfaces is hard enough to see, but F-105F 63-8287 (photo 116), with 'wraparound', is harder still to make out. Both these aircraft belonged to the 466th TFS/419th TFW, Air Force Reserve, and are seen here at Hill AFB in October 1983. (Douglas R. Tachauer)

117. Framed by the nose of an F-105D, an F-105F Thunderchief (63-8361) from the 466th TFS/419th TFW, Air Force Reserve, is seen during a visit to Toronto, Canada in September 1983. (Douglas R. Tachauer)

118. With its radome open, F-105G Thunderchief 63-8328 of the 128th TFS/116th TFW, Georgia ANG, looks ready to eat. In fact this Wild Weasel is undergoing a last-minute maintenance check prior to taxiing out, 20 August 1982. (Douglas R. Tachauer)

118▼

▲119　▼120

119. The 'Thud' took off and landed fast. This F-105D, 60-0535, is seen low over the Kansas countryside near McConnell AFB with 'everything hanging out'. (USAF)

120. The parched Arizona sun shines on the hulks of Thunderchiefs which have reached the end of the line. F-105D 61-0071, formerly of the 149th TFS/192nd TFG, Virginia ANG, has had sealant applied and has received storage number FK049 at the Military Aircraft Storage and Disposition Center (MASDC) at Davis-Monthan AFB near Tucson. The photograph was taken in April 1983. (Philip A. Tachauer)

121. Another Georgia Air National G-model, also seen on 20 August 1982, is aircraft 62-4422, at Dobbins AFB. The aircraft carries miniscule BDU-33 practice bomblets on a centreline multiple ejector rack. (Douglas R. Tachauer)

▲ 122

122. The last Thunderchief ever to fly with the Air National Guard, F-105F 63-8299, with notations in yellow lettering to indicate the final flight of the type. This Georgia ANG aircraft was flown from Dobbins AFB, Georgia, to NAS Patuxent River, Maryland, by Maj. Duff Greene on 25 May 1983, to mark the 'Thud's retirement. An orange peach, symbol of the state of Georgia, appeared beneath the canopy, highlighted in yellow with green leaves and a black stem. (Donald Spering/AIR)

123. The Air Force Reserve eventually retired its last 'Thud' not long after the Air National Guard ceased to operate the type. The all-time historical gathering of Thunderchiefs, however, came not at the very end but a few years earlier, on 12 July 1980, with the first flight ever of all five F-105 Thunderchief production models together. Furthermore, each of the five airframes had a claim to

fame. F-105G 63-8285 of the 35th TFW ('WW' tail code), leading the flight, had earlier, as an F-105F, been the first two-seat Thunderchief in combat, in 1964; F-105F 62-4413, of the 192nd TFG, Virginia ANG, in the upper rear position, had been the first production F-105F officially delivered to the US Air Force, in 1963; F-105D ('Thunderstick II') 60-0490 of the 301st TFW, Air Force Reserve, upper centre, had been the last F-105D to fly a combat mission in South-East Asia, in 1970; F-105D 62-4372 of the 507th TFG, Air Force Reserve, seen below the flight leader, had been the first F-105 to achieve 6,000 flying hours, in 1978; and F-105B 57-5776 of the 108th TFG, New Jersey ANG, the lowest aircraft in this view, had been the first production F-105B, in 1958. This unusual five-ship formation, which used the call-sign 'Thud Flight', is seen over George AFB, California. (Via Marty J. Isham)

▼ 123